D1603891

SMUGGLER

Nicholas Fillmore

iambic Books

The events and conversations in this book have been set down to the best of the author's ability, although some names and details have been changed to protect the privacy of individuals.

First paperback edition January 2019

Library of Congress Control Number: 2018913389

ISBN 978-0-578-40348-9 (paperback)
ISBN 978-0-578-40349-6 (ebook)

Printed in the U.S.A.

published by iambic Books
Kailua, Hawaii
www.iambicbooks.com

For L.

We are all exceptional cases. We all want to appeal against something! Each of us insists on being innocent at all cost, even if he has to accuse the whole human race and heaven itself.

—Albert Camus, *The Fall*

Contents

Part One

Part Two

There's no room in the drug culture for amateurs.
　　　　　　　　　　—Hunter S. Thompson

Part One

Marabout

The highway, a graded red clay road raised right on top of itself, went north into the interior, through the bush—around armed checkpoints, beyond the Africa of hotel bars and *jelly cocos*, into an immensity.

Red dust settled in the wake of the four cars speeding along.

Three hours later we turned down a road to a little village snowbound in noon heat. A stand of old trees and some wooden shacks made a center square. Then the land fell away, branches scraped the sides of the car and the road disappeared. We stopped and got out, the Africans replacing *kufis* and throwing sleeves of kaftans over their shoulders. Someone pointed to a thicket, and we clambered down an embankment into a gulley of thorn bushes and entered a low, red mud hut.

A figure naked to the waste was squatting on the floor, staring into a little pink plastic mirror with a cocoon bound to the front. Then he was staring into my face. Then the mirror. Back and forth—drinking clear liquid (African gin) from a scarred glass. As I squatted down and looked into his eyes, vaguely aware of the impertinence, something crawled out from behind his expression, flickered there for an instant and was gone. Then he was all lines, the geometry of indifference.

At the center of the hut an altar of mud and feathers and wax and bones picked at your attention.

The Nigerians, long black hands floating in front of them, sat on a low bench against the wall, impatient to find out what had happened to their shipment of heroin. And all around the hut children jostled for position in little windows, their blank, smooth faces revealing nothing.

The marabout, an oracle, tossed a handful of cowrie shells in a metal pan, considered their arrangement and tossed them again. Then he began to speak.

After a moment, one of the Nigerians interrupted. "The bag," he said, gently.

The marabout murmured something.

"The bag!" A Nigerian with designer sunglasses shouted in English.

The marabout repeated himself.

An explosion of voices ensued. "The bag, the *bag!*" everyone shouted.

The marabout spoke a different dialect of Yoruba. People shouted in French, in English.

In the midst of this, an image of the airport terminal rose up in my mind: Shaky, hand-held shot of shoes, suitcases—the frantic search for the bag. Standing in a phone booth, chopping the air with my hand, talking, talking, muffled by glass….

Suddenly the events of my life were so strange, all I could do was register the details, camera-like—the facts: *I am in a hut in a village somewhere along the Nigerian border. I am thirty-one years old. (I'm sorry, L; I didn't mean it to come to this.)*

Claire

I remember a conversation with a young English Professor one late spring day before I became a heroin smuggler. Slogging across the quad after a rainstorm, that kind of spring morning you get upstate when everything changes, he'd admonished me about "the writing life": "If you're foolish enough to throw your life away," he said.

It was like everything stopped in that instant, and though we went our separate directions, to dining hall and office, some trace of us remained there in the rain contemplating that proposition: To throw one's life away. What is the attraction of that? It is a young man's conceit, no doubt, presupposing a knowledge of all the world's wasted effort. A first cigarette, tasting of honey and lye....

Afterwards, I studied with a famous poet. There was a moment, too, when words and the rhythms of words themselves seemed a perfected kind of existence.

Later, but not so much later, I got involved in crime. It happened the usual way: I was broke and available, doing unpaid work for a desktop publisher and waiting tables for the umpteenth time. I lived with my girlfriend in a dusty Northampton apartment that let long, yellow sunlight into the room. L was finishing up college.

Days off we drove up to the mountains or Boston or the Cape, my Ford Granada rollicking along on old springs toward some final destination that was not yet clear. A close reading of my *vita* might have told another story. Of course it could have foretold any number of things. I was a good prep school boy, somewhat out of my league and sorely lacking in "cultural capital"; threw off personas in college like clothes: urban cowboy, hippie, punk, poet; and wrote some things later in grad school....

In fact, I'd recently been fired from the restaurant—those days I was always getting fired from restaurants—and been scraping rent together, subsisting on pasta and video rentals and free drinks. Not that I wasn't happy in my way. I didn't know any better; I was in love.

L and I strolled through town holding hands under hundred-year-old Maples; lay on the couch watching movies; ate, hiked, browsed and day-tripped, spending our coins one at a time.

We'd recognized each other at first glance with a start one rainy June morning in the *A House* alley in Provincetown and despite working at the same café all summer barely managed more than a few words, a couple innuendos, not out of any exalted notions about romantic love; we simply didn't know what to say.

The next year we fell in together right away all quickened breath and balled fists and for a whole summer ran in and out of waves on the long spit of sand on the outer Cape. (That slow burn formed part of our personal myth; like all lovers, we idealized ourselves.)

Then L returned to Western Mass and broke up with me, twenty-four and fully come into her own, and I returned to Hartford to lick wounds and compose strange, macabre poems in my bedroom at my parents' house.

That winter I half-heartedly went from job to job—they told me I needed to take a shave at The Courant—and wound up working at an all-night Greek diner across from the train station serving scrambled eggs to late night bar patrons. The cook, a crack addict who slept in a cot in the basement, scampered up the stairs when you rang a bell.

In the spring I showed back up in Provincetown in black jeans and cowboy boots, that catch in the throat each time you returned to town. It was like walking in in the middle of a film: Fabulous characters in eyeliner and beards cavorted up and down Commercial Street. Artists who'd been working for a week straight staggered out of garages high on fumes. And fishermen lacquered in blood and fish scales clutched at bar rails, roaring at the ceiling. Of course the whole thing was really about sex.

Not yet 30, I was old news already. Gone were college days I turned the heads of all the old queens lounging on the meat rack in front of Town Hall or made waitresses blush. Lacking anything resembling "buzz" I held on like a winded boxer, figuring if I could just go the distance some credit might fall to me. Mostly I hung on.

L and I reconciled, and in the fall we moved to Northampton to set up house in an apartment in some old row houses. If Provincetown was the place you came to when you couldn't run any further, the Pioneer Valley was where you dug in: a farming community built on silts drained from great mountains to the north.

Historically a hotbed of rural dissent to the politics of Boston, it attracted political liberals to its five colleges.

L's classes resumed. I haunted bookstores, biked out to secret reservoirs and raced down hills shivering in the wind; hung about the town with its lovely pink brick and ersatz New York; made some abortive attempts to write poetry.—

Then Claire showed up. I knew Claire from Provincetown and was surprised to see her in Northampton. She and L lived together the summer L and I started dating. Those first weeks I'd see them dancing every night at the *A House* in jeans and T-shirts, sleeves rolled up on their biceps, captains' caps and lipstick.

After last call we'd ride our bikes to Herring Cove to go skinny-dipping in inky darkness, sudden kelp beds, swirling phosphorescence. One night we all went back to their apartment.

L fell asleep in Claire's bed and Claire and I continued to drink and to smoke cigarettes. Claire seemed like me to be searching for a narrative. Lacking another material she talked about architecture school in Boston. Artforum magazine. Europe. I couldn't quite make out what she was getting at. Her words, cadences, pauses had the shape of an argument, yet lacked any discernible premise.

"The people who are doing that kind of work," she said with conviction, "are doing something new. The art world in general…."

Claire sprawled out on the bed between L and me. I turned politely away; in the sorting the following morning kissed L….

I was sitting on the stoop of a Northampton bakery drinking coffee when Claire came striding down the street with a young guy and girl in tow. She'd just moved to Northampton and seemed to be chasing after one or both young things; had wormed her way into their affairs and was orchestrating things to her liking.

Claire stood there on the brick sidewalk, a riot of blonde hair, making Harpo Marx faces.— And whether she figured the whole thing out in that instant, or it came to her in pieces, I don't know.

"What are *you* doing here?" she said.

"I'm a freshman at Smith College," I said.

"And I'm the big bad wolf."

We all hung out a few times in Northampton. On one occasion Claire was with the boy, the next time she had the girl, intent on making a show of it there on the couch.

L was up early mornings to do fieldwork in wetlands around Amherst; I was out drinking with restaurant people till closing. Each night I'd run into Claire in one of a half-dozen local pubs.

Drinking magnified our complaint. Claire wanted money and she wanted attention, and she wanted to be right. One of those seemingly indestructible people who suddenly reveal a maudlin side (and the next day are themselves again), she composed herself not in sentences or in paragraphs but in chapters, a southerner, after all, a Cincinnatian; she was telling a story, and she had decided to tell it to me.

Claire had a younger sister named Hester who lived in Chicago, kind of a witchy girl by all accounts, a redhead who'd been spend-ing a lot of time abroad and was involved with an African, Claire said vaguely. She was starting a magazine called *Nun Civa Orcus* about voodoo and other arcane preoccupations. I didn't know what any of it meant. Clearly, Claire held her in awe. Yet the more Claire talked about Hester, the murkier the pic-ture she made. It seemed that in trying to solve the occult mystery of her sister, Claire had somehow raveled herself and me in it. (Months later they'd have it out in the middle of the street in Paris, a couple of termagants flapping and tearing at one another.)

Not so much with words but with gestures, Claire hinted that a destiny awaited us. There was talk of the magazine and of travel—of busting out of the narrow confines of our lives, the modesty of our twenties. I sat and listened and stared into a drink.

Over the next few months the magazine started to materialize. Hester and her friend Barry sent photographs, and I began to design a pamphlet and wrangle copy into a coherent form at the DTP shop in Amherst. And Claire and I continued to conspire in bar and booth.

One night, satisfied with her dramatic build-up, Claire confessed that Hester was smuggling drugs for a Nigerian. And my heart sank. So this was the dark matter that invisibly shaped our conversations. And the more she went on about this Nigerian she referred to as *Alhaji,* the less enticing it all seemed. Of course I didn't really know Claire.

I didn't walk away, either. Instead, I hung around to see what was going to happen next. Rent was due. (*Christ, rent.* In the last three months I'd hauled my old Chevette out of a field behind L's old apartment and sold it for a few hundred dollars, then collected the insurance after somebody dinged the Granada, then borrowed from my parents. It looked like my string of luck was run out.) So one winter day Claire and I took off for Chicago.

What I told L was ostensibly true: I was going to help start this magazine. Here were the brochures, of which I was a little proud; and the poster that I'd sent to art colleges around the country calling for work; and half-believing it myself, a manifesto.

L looked at me doubtfully. "The rent," she said.

I'd get the rent, damn it. Maybe more than that.—— You were good as long as you stayed within the bounds of law, right?

*

After a straight twelve-hour drive Claire and I pulled up to the apartment, the first floor of a three story walk-up in Logan Square a few blocks from some gang turf.

Hester was away, but the roommate, Mickey, expected us. With his whiffle haircut, his sharp teeth and narrow-set eyes, he looked like a small, predatory animal. He circled you like a dog. No doubt he was in the habit of sizing up couriers, but Claire wanted to keep him at bay, so I played dumb and stared up at the ceiling while she and Mickey spoke in shorthand of this and that.

It reminded me of scoring pot in high school all those years ago with my friend Chico: pulling up to some run-down apartment complex and slinking up poured concrete steps, hands in pockets, to meet the local dealer, a trade school dropout … but because I wasn't "cool" just yet being left in the living room while they went into the back bedroom to weigh an ounce; afterwards, because everyone was invariably an amateur and pothead, a bag would be produced, pot cleaned of copious stems and seeds on the obligatory double-live album cover and a joint rolled and smoked because it was cool after all, it was fun, and while it may even have been business, it involved certain rites.

Later Mickey made dinner. We ate at a big table with heavy, dark chairs. Against one wall was an antique sideboard. The windows were covered with dark jacquard pattern drapes; shabby oriental carpet on the floor.

We drank several bottles of red wine. That REM song was on the radio: *"Andy are you goofing on Elvis? Hey, baby. Are we having fun?"*

"Oh, my God, I went to this place called *Manhole* last night," Mickey was saying.

"Did you wear a condom?" Claire said.

"Did I wear a condom?" Mickey said.

I got drunk enough to brave the night in Hester's room, a windowless cell with a mattress on the floor, a tangle of sheets and an empty wine goblet—a postcard of the Sacred Heart of Jesus stapled to the wall above the bed.

The next morning we had breakfast and coffee—Mickey was well-provisioned—and were just getting down to business, when the phone rang. Claire took the call in another room. Then Mickey went in after her. A half hour later Claire came out of the room, bags packed, dressed.

"See you when I get back," she said. Then she left.

Mickey and I continued to dodge one another for the next few hours. That evening we were watching TV when he pulled out a piece of tin foil. "You want to smoke some heroin?" he asked, very matter-of-fact.

I'd used once before; just a kid out of school, my experiments in "the dark night of the soul" wobbling into unsafe orbit, I'd shot up with an ex-con named Cosmos in the bathroom of a club I worked at. I remember the shot hitting me and staggering to the bar and laying my head in my arms. Next thing some lovely punk rock girl was worrying over me out on the street after closing.

All that stuff, the *femme fatale* posturing of my twenties, was behind me now. Alcohol was my heroin, a benefaction. After three drinks a weight rolled off and my breathing would ease, as if I'd been running all day long—as if I'd been excused or absolved or unburdened or *disburthened*. Problem was another, darker impulse always rose up, demanding to be endured.

In fact, I yearned for an experience—to try myself on some other, absolute scale of values, maybe. Lacking imagination, I'd make some half-hearted stab: Get in a car with the wrong people. Shoot heroin. Of course such gestures are fatal precisely because they're insincere.

I angled the foil and held a flame to the grains of heroin till they caramelized like sugar and a black thread of smoke unspooled, which you chased with a straw, a brief sensation of heat going in. I guess I got high; after using a needle there didn't seem to be much point doing it otherwise. We watched TV, entranced by a Star Trek episode, a race of cyborgs trying to assimilate humanity.

The next morning I spread all my magazine stuff out on the dining room table and tried to come up with a plan. There was a briefcase filled with brochures, ad rates and artwork, and the idea of a magazine called *Nun Civa Orcus*, another of Hester's attempts at self-concealment, no doubt—a name … the magazine equivalent of calling your kid Hercules or Jasper or Mauna Kea or Fuckhead. At least I could pitch galleries.

Within a week a handful of people had responded to the want ad in the Tribune and we went barnstorming (on a strictly commission basis) through the Gold Coast and North Side. Each morning we'd meet at a coffee shop to rehearse our lines, then make our sales calls.

The first place, an impossibly stylish mid-western gallery owner seemed to tolerate my physical presence only with a great deal of effort.

"Nun *what?*" she said, fairly spitting the words out.

I handed her a brochure and walked over to a painting she'd been straightening and pretended to study it.

She tossed the papers on her desk and studied her manicure impassively.

"Norman Mailer is contributing to our first issue," I lied.

"Who?"

"Robert Hughes."

"I don't know who that is."

*

I returned to Mass feeling defeated. Claire showed up several weeks later, paid me a thousand dollars in cash and told me about her trip.

She'd been to Paris and Brussels, and then to Benin, West Africa to meet with the other couriers at the boss's house in Cotonou. They'd swallowed condoms containing heroin, flown back to Chicago, "harvested" the heroin and collected the proceeds. Would I like to join in?

The Story of My Life

I must have known the answer all along, so caught up with my quarrel with the world I hardly gave it a thought—as if in closing one's eyes and throwing blind one might avoid questions altogether.

The plan was to go to Europe, grab some jackets with heroin sewn into the lining—no swallowing—and come back through Customs. Just like that.

I told L that I was going back out to Chicago to work on the magazine. She was busy with classes. Rent was paid. Food in the fridge. Car gassed up. "See you in a week," I said—an understatement, a habit, L said, I had of "sugar-coating" things.

Claire and I flew to Chicago and checked into the Blackstone Hotel, a Beaux-Arts edifice on Michigan and Balboa with comfortable, outdated rooms and a view of the fountain in Grant Park. After dropping off our bags we took the elevator back down to the lobby and walked through a big, empty ballroom and under a curving staircase to the street-level bar. It was early Friday evening. The place was crowded: guys in turtlenecks, blousy businesswomen, folks who looked like they were making their way around to the jazz clubs—a whole new grown-up city life.

We ordered B&Bs and slouched into a curve of the bar, ordered more drinks and shouted at each other for an hour or so about nothing at all.

"Could you ever imagine you'd be involved in something like this?" Claire said.

"No," I said, kind of dazzled by everything: the scale, the hour. The Blackstone had once been grand, "the hotel of Presidents," but now had a distinctly louche atmosphere: Black marble. Lock boxes behind the front desk.

"This is the hotel we use."

It was a local, Chicago hotel. Not some fucking Marriott.

"Don't let on if you recognize anyone."

"Huh?"

"There could be people here right now."

This only inflamed my imagination. The whole trip—standing on the street, sitting in a restaurant, brushing my teeth—I half expected Africans to come sauntering around the corner at any moment to transact a drug deal. Or the cops to come rushing in. Of course I didn't know anyone to begin with and wondered idly what an African heroin dealer might look like—imagining them in pairs in codpieces and fool's caps, mirrored sunglasses and velvet smoking jackets in an intricate *pas de deux*.

In the course of my ruminations it got dark. The lights came on in the Park. A gust of wind came off the lake, jangling traffic signals. The moment had passed, but we stayed on like late-comers drinking double-fisted.—

In a way that hotel's fate was tied to our own. All those downtown revelers disappeared just as our own luck disappeared, the whole story-like sense of reality that enveloped us and encouraged us to believe that events were being narrated somehow, guiding us unerringly to a predestined end, dismantled, packed in boxes and hauled away.

I was still drunk the next morning as we drove around the departures terminal at Midway looking for our gate. On the second lap it occurred to Claire that we had the wrong airport; our flight was leaving *O'Hare*. After a brutal cross-town cab ride, spinning and sweating and trying to focus on some point a mile high, we found Air France and checked in. We were sitting in a bar in the departure lounge nursing beers when an announcement came over the intercom: "Passenger Nicholas Fillmore, report to the Air France ticketing desk."

—The story of my life. Either I skated through, heedless of the dangers all around, or someone threw a rock into a crowd and hit me.

On the long walk back to the ticketing counter I imagined all kinds of bad things: agents in trim, dark suits, bright lights, handcuffs—more trouble in an endless succession of troubles. Ever since I could remember I was getting in trouble.

When I was just nine or ten my friend Jimmy and I stole a birthday present. It was one of those neighborhood affairs with prize bags and pin-the-tail-on-the-donkey and hot dogs and a cake. While everyone was focused on the kid unwrapping gifts, Jimmy coolly stuck this little orange submarine down his trunks.

Afterwards, we went across the street to his house and put the submarine in a tub of water in the yard. A tiny battery-powered propeller drove the thing in an aimless, dispirited fashion, like a dying goldfish. Then Jimmy went inside.

As I ducked under the hemlocks into our yard my mother came out the back door at a run.

"What did you do with Sandy Berger's submarine?" she said thickly.

"I didn't do anything."

She slapped me hard across the face.

"What did you do with it?"

"I didn't do anything."

She slapped me again.

"What did you do?"

"Nothing."

Slap. "Don't lie to me."

"Alright," I said.

She looked at me.

"Jimmy took it."

So Jimmy and I returned the sub and apologized to Berger and his mother, a giraffe-like woman who looked tenderly down at her son as if to silently affirm some sad truth about the world. Whereas my mother was merely, justifiably mortified.

Jimmy and I were altar boys. Jimmy's mother, who'd gone to seminary, taught CCD classes on Wednesday nights. Over the years, I assailed her catechism on all sides. Then she'd kick me out of class. Jimmy's father, a gym teacher and agnostic with a bald head and penguine physique, lurked in the shadows at the top of the basement stairs.

"Get over here you little schmo," he'd say in his South Shore Boston accent and deftly roll onto his back and put you in a scissors hold or complicated leg-lock that you spent the next thirty minutes trying to get out of. You'd here guys thrashing around on the floor of the living room and kitchen above class.

In time my attention wandered to the girls in class. There were two on those Wednesday nights: Kathleen Flaherty and Laurie Connor—and a substitute teacher lactating prodigiously in a low-cut blouse.

"… Oh, not *boys*," their new big sister quipped, and the troika threw their heads back in salacious laughter, molars showing.

"What do *you* want?" Kathleen said, catching me looking at her. Her dark eyes flashed.

I didn't know what I wanted (I did, of course), but something else, infinitely lonely, stirred down inside me that wanted only to bury its face in all those curls. It was immodest, surely, and the girls, who seemed to know this about us already, kept a sensible distance.

After class we were all running around some big Spruce pines across the street. The grass was that deep green before the first frost. Our breath hung on the night air. Laurie Connor came running around a tree, laughing, I came around the other way and put my forearms up like a blocking tackle and crashed right into her. She lay on the grass, a look of shock on her face, arms folded her across her chest, struggling for breath.

And I stood there feeling like hell: Wrong and wronged, all my worst instincts laid bare. Not merely bad, but stupid. I'd mixed up everything.

It would be a long time, longer than most perhaps, until adolescence blew over, and so I lay a-hull, battered by the forces of my own psyche, no girlfriends, no snug harbor, no relief from the harangue of the self; just the longing and the self-loathing and sports….

Baseball transposed desire onto a field.

When I stepped into the batter's box everything else disappeared. My uncertainty about what I thought, my shyness around girls, my essential ignorance of the ways of the world all vanished, and I floated in a calm, blue void, hands quiet, mind clear....

Spring of my senior year we already had the league championship clinched, and with a game remaining, I was a base hit away from the school record. I was sitting in Freddy Schwartz's room smoking a cigarette. Freddy was in the shower, cutting class. We were essentially done with school, enjoying those last long spring days, free and in full possession of ourselves before we all went off to college to find whatever destiny awaited us.

Dean Meyers popped his bespectacled head in the door, interrupting my reverie. A grey-blue nimbus of smoke hung in the air—long ash on the cigarette held absently between my fingers.

"Nick, aren't you on the baseball team? Athletes aren't allowed to smoke. I'm afraid you can't play in the game this afternoon."—A tidy syllogism, like he had the goddamn thing prepared.

That afternoon I went into the locker room, pulled on my uniform and cleats, blacked my eyes and clattered across the parking lot to the field. Coach Beebe was raking the pitcher's mound.

"Dean Meyers told me you were smoking. You can't play today," he said, passing a handkerchief over his bald, shaved head. Beebe was a scholar and eccentric in the grand old tradition, and expert on the Weimar Republic. He carried a cane, which he waved in the air at insolent students.

"No, it was Freddy Schwartz's cigarette. It was all a mistake," I said. "I cleared it with Dean Meyers."

What was I thinking?

My first at bat the pitcher threw a fastball. About half way to the plate the ball suddenly came into focus and seemed to hang there for an instant, and I hit it spang on the seams, neither topspin nor backspin, just a hard, dead flight over the left fielder's head, one hop off the fence and into the record books.

Next day I was lying on the grass after lunch enjoying myself when someone said, "Your father." I looked up. My father was coming across the quad in long strides, just forty-two, black hair and thickening Marine's build.

"You'd better come with me," he said.

Sitting against the wall of the Boys' Dean's Office were Dean Meyers, Coach Beebe and Glover Howe, who for twenty years or more had functioned as the school's unofficial day-to-day conscience (and concierge).

"I was surprised," Dean Meyers said, opening the proceeding, "to hear what a good game you played yesterday, after you'd been banned for smoking."

Well, he had me there. A wonder of logic, the man was.

"... But what's more troubling is that you lied to Mr. Beebe. We take lying very seriously at Loomis Chaffee."

Myers rearranged himself on his chair and looked at Coach Beebe, then at Mr. Howe, who nodded for him to continue.

"You know, a few years back there were two boys in here. One had been in a fight. The other told a lie regarding the incident. Do you know which one was expelled?"

I said the one who lied.

"The one who told a lie," Dean Meyers said.

I nodded gravely.

"In addition to that, Coach Beebe tells me that you missed a work assignment last week. That gives you six unexcused absences. I'm afraid I'll have to call the Disciplinary Committee."

Mr. Howe ran his fingers through a profusion of grey hair as he followed the warp of Meyers' argument.

A preemptive noise came from my father's throat.

I objected vigorously to the "deep six" and realizing I'd mortally offended Coach Beebe, threw myself on his mercy. In fact I was sorry as hell for causing so much grief to everyone. Looking around the room at these adults unanimous in their concern for my welfare, I felt like a shit.

In the end I would not join that honor roll of fellows who had been rusticated for drugs and sex and general mayhem and whose names—Nigel Palmer, Peter Roth—passed into school lore, invoking awe and respect; but walking back onto campus the Monday after my three-day suspension I felt half an inch taller—looked, from a certain mirror-angle, half-dangerous. In truth I was already beginning to mount some upward or outward trajectory, though not yet at escape velocity. That would require other crimes.

At the Air France ticketing counter at O'Hare, an agent smiled and handed over my passport, which I'd forgotten. As I walked back to the lounge studying the picture of myself—twenty years old on a month-long *Eurail* trip, a real ingénue—the whole idea of what we were up to sank in and all the tension I'd been holding rose up and I ran into the men's room and vomited into a urinal.

Drowning

In Paris we checked into *Hotel Saint André des Arts* in the 6th arrondissement, my room just a little closet under the gables. Famished, I bought a half chicken and baguette at a street market and set off to picnic somewhere, walking one street, then another, looking for a place to sit. Every inch seemed to be taken. *Saint Germain des Pres,* shrouded in a mist, lay in one direction. *Point Neuf* in another. I hesitated, then plunged ahead like a man swarmed by bees, finally found a stone bench under a little ornamental cherry tree in a tiny park at the end of a street and greedily tore at the meat and the bread with bare hands.

Walking back on St. Germain I passed The *Deux Magots, tout Paris* in Ray Bans and Armani, me with crummy shoes and greasy hands moodily smoking on the sidewalk, a provincial newly arrived in the capitol of the world—a tourist, a terrorist, a platypus fetched out of his pool and deposited there on the curb for all to see, making a thin, fearful noise like air escaping.

How is it, I still wonder, that I simultaneously saw myself a sophisticate and naif? Considered myself a reasonable person, willing to chuck all reason aside? It seems that I had a talent for compartmentalizing aspects of myself. Maybe smuggling was an attempt, by obliterating all distinctions, by stretching them as far as they'd go, to integrate those selves....

Claire took me to a chic Paris salon where I got a facial and manicure because it was high time to throw off small-town fustiness. The cosmetician, a handsome French woman, abandoned her comedone extractor and went at me with her thumbnails, her ample bosom up against my shoulder as she energetically squeezed and palpated.

I bought a pair of brown shoes on sale on *Champs Elysees* and a tie with sober foulard and cursing God in his distant heaven flung my old shoes into the river.

Back at the hotel I tied a half-Windsor knot in the mirror, tossed my head back and spoke aloud: *"Je voudrais le steak frites, et donnez-nous une bouteille du Beaujolais Nouveau ... Je suis Americain, je travaille comme editeur dans un magazine d'art ... Quel beau temps nous avons...."*

A day later we took the train to Belgium. At the station in Brussels we met Barry and Paul, Hester's friends. Barry danced around like a little dog. Paul, his master, was considerably more aloof. This was his trip. Paul was senior courier at the moment.

An esthete and executor of his dead lover's paintings, the story went that he'd fallen into smuggling to pay for his dying boyfriend's medical expenses, which in those early AIDS days was a labor of love merely. Now he stuck with smuggling to curate Rowan's work. I envied his *reasons*.

He seemed to take my presence as a personal affront. As Barry gamboled back and forth between Claire and me, Paul affected not to notice my presence, which struck me as fairly pissy, if not a little rude.

We walked single file down the street from the station: Paul, then Barry, then Claire and me, Claire angling like a distance runner for the inside track. They made me wait down on the street while they ransacked an apartment Paul owed back rent on. For whatever reason, the organizational ethos involved a certain amount of hazing.— Claire told me how Piss-Paul had thrown her prized motorcycle boots out the window of a cab on the last trip and how Alhaji glee-fully stuffed them all full of dubious African cookery to stretch their stomachs in preparation for swallowing heroin.

My especial torture was going to be death-by-waiting. Left to my own macabre imaginings I looked up and down *Rue Lemonnier* whose gothic facades did nothing to quell my terror, which by that point was screaming out loud, it being one thing to wade into battle, another to await orders behind enemy lines.

We checked into a hotel in a little Arab neighborhood nearby. It was Sunday afternoon. Some kids were kicking a ball on the side-walk. A radio played. Flowers spilled from an iron railing on a high granite wall across the Boulevard. We waited and waited, clean sun-light all about the room.

Until Alhaji called, we had to sit tight.

At least that's how Paul ran things.

I squirted three eyedroppers of valerian into a glass of water, drank it down and stared at the ceiling, suddenly quite aware of the hydraulic workings of my heart.

Unable to stand the torment any longer, I begged my way out of the room and went down to the street. *Rai* pumped out of a corner bar, exuberant Algerian pop music. Inside, a bunch of mid-dle-aged Arab men were dancing to Cheb Khaled. I ordered a *raqi*, drank it, ordered another. The men raised their glasses. I raised mine and danced.

The next morning everyone disappeared to collect the jackets. Piss-Paul left right away, loathe to inconvenience himself in any way. Then Barry trotted after him. Claire gave me two jackets with solemn instructions to catch a train later that afternoon. Then she left.

There was just enough time to shower and pack and get myself to Central Station. The train was crowded. A motley group sat on overstuffed duffle bags in between the cars. I wedged myself into an open seat next to them. Unable to read or sleep or do anything else, I looked around the car at the other passengers, trying to guess their secrets:

Which one was alcoholic?

Which from an abusive home?

Which had a suitcase full of drugs?

At the French border the cops came on the train and a thorough-looking gendarme stepped into our car.

In the harsh glare of the moment I understood that we're always attempting to pass ourselves off in one way or another (with the exception of the impossibly stupid and well-born, who go through life with apparent ease). And as the cop's glance swept over me I felt my lips curl into an obsequious grin—a gruesome imitation of someone trying to "act natural."

The cop looked right past me, and for perhaps the first time in my life I understood the advantage of being white and middle class ... if by "middle class" one meant being possessed of the belief that abstract concepts of opportunity and fairness applied to one, I was middle class.

An hour later the train pulled into *Gare du Nord*. I took the stairs down into the Metro and came out at the *Odeon* stop; walked down a short street and ran up the worn stairs of the hotel. In my little room I shoved the suitcase and jackets, lumpy with packets of heroin in the lining, under the creaky little bed, stripped off my sweaty clothes and slept until dinner.

Later I set to work on my cover story. I'd decided to pose as a magazine editor and for the next week busied myself at the *Salon de Mars* and the left bank galleries, tentatively chatting with gallery owners, looking at pictures and stuffing brochures into a folder.

In my free time I smoked Galoises, walked despondently about *Ile de Cité*—the spot I imagined Hugo's Javert to have thrown himself into the Seine; wandered boulevards, side streets, alleys narrowing to medieval dimensions, pursued by an argument: whatever else might be said of my decision to smuggle heroin, it was perfectly clear to me that I was on a fool's errand—not out of any overt design to be a fool, of course, but to feel life up close, hold my hand to the hotplate of experience, a fool all the same.

On the night before my departure I drank giant raspberry beers at an empty outdoor café, marveling in a happy moment of forgetfulness at the buds of trees wheeling over my head; threw my last Galois into the gutter and stumbled home to bed.

The next morning I sat in front of my suitcase obsessively packing and unpacking, wanting nothing so much as to be rid of the evidence. I tried on one of the jackets: two sizes small and padded like an Hussar. The cuffs came up well above the wrist. The whole thing bulged and sagged: a sack suit cut inartfully out of material for an Egyptian banker. I guessed if it got to the point they were going through your suitcase you were pretty much done for anyway.

Claire came into the room and goggled at me.

"You're not supposed to wear it!" she said.

"Hide in plain sight, no?"

"My father always rolls his jackets inside out. That's how all the executives do it so it doesn't get all wrinkled."

I turned the jacket inside out, the lining a lurid pistachio-candy cane stripe, folded it and rolled it as tightly as I could and jammed it into a corner of the suitcase.

"Put some shirts over it," Claire said. "Put your dirty underwear on top of it."

"I'm not sure there's room. Maybe I'll just leave it…."

"I wouldn't want to lose one of those."

"What would happen?"

"Nobody ever lost one yet."

"But if someone did?"

"I don't think you want to find out."

"Yeah, but if they did."

Claire pointed her index finger at her temple and jerked her head back, making a stooge-face. "Is that what you want to hear?"

"Yeah," I said.

Later that morning I carried my bags through check-in at de Gaulle, navigated the labyrinth of escalators to the gate and boarded the plane, careful to avoid being seen with the others.

Once or twice I looked up and caught Barry's eye by accident and looked quickly away. Of course if one of us went down, we all would; it wasn't difficult to connect the dots, since Hester had bought all the tickets together. Right then, however, my main concern was my "story"; but as I looked down at my improbable shoes and the big, square, black attaché case I'd bought, it occurred to me how unlikely a business passenger I looked.

Anyway, I was prepared for their questions. Each night in Paris Claire and Barry had grilled me: *What is the purpose of your visit? How long were you in Paris? Did you travel outside of the country? Did you meet anyone? Are you carrying any bags that don't belong to you?* And of course the unthinkable: *would you open your bag, please? Are these your things?*

I'd finally arranged my "things" thus and abandoned myself to the illusion of purposeful activity, forward motion. As long as one moved forward, one felt safe. As long as one felt safe, one *was* safe.

The rest of the flight I tried not to think too much, shoved down the little stirrings of conscience till what remained was a low-grade regret, a heartburn.

It was a familiar sensation, as it seemed to me I'd spent a good deal of my youth running like hell from trouble, laughing at the incredulity of grownups—as if they didn't remember the irresistible urge to lob petards at the sanctimony of adults.

One time I tossed a snowball through some guy's car window. Amid a gravelly whoosh of brakes, this teenager in crushed velvet tuxedo leapt out of his Mustang, violently brushing snow from his lapel. He looked wildly about and seeing us took half a step toward the curb—my "friends" to my great disappointment having hauled me out of hiding and offered me up to the angry, mustachioed teen-god. He hesitated then, seeing the snow bank, unwilling to sully his shoes, these zippered ankle boots, which drew our simultaneous attention. Seeing my admiration for his footwear seemed to abate his anger. In fact, if I'm not mistaken, he turned his heel out a quarter of an inch. Then blushed. Then sputtered a bit, then flexed three or four times and patched out, and I slinked home, none the wiser.

Another time ... linked in memory with inexpressible sadness as one of life's great truths bore in on me, that despite our fondest depictions of ourselves as Augustines and Robespierres we are mostly just reluctant participants in life's cruel one-acts, dupes at best ... we destroyed these melons.

A bunch of us, probably just seven, eight, nine-years old, were cutting through the woods one late afternoon when we came upon a garden plot. It was mid-August, a couple of weeks before school. The sun already had that autumnal slant, and the melons lay on their sides, ripe and round. And for a moment we just stood there, stupefied. Then someone picked a melon, broke a branch off a tree and jabbed the melon onto it.

I understood, even with my child's mind, the grotesqueness of it. We impaled melon after melon, stolidly, stupidly twisting and twisting as gobs of flesh fell from the ripe fruit, before unceremoniously chucking it all in a pile.

That evening there was a knock on the door. The owner of the plot, perplexed more than outraged, was making the rounds of the neighborhood to confer with parents. I could hear everything from upstairs: the initial note of disbelief in my parents' voices, their objection; then because I was a year or two younger than the big boys and out of some deference to my supposed lack of moral development, the adults speaking in hushed tones as if they might disturb some delicate chrysalis of thought, though in fact I understood what was going on the whole time, understood the wantonness of what we'd done, the pointlessness of it—they let me off without a word.

It must have been a formative moment. Time and again afterwards I saw fit to play dumb, make like I didn't get what was going on. Which is not to say that I didn't groan inwardly. But something had begun to grow up in me, or rather *between* me and life. For to receive one's just punishment is to feel life up close.

Land edged into view on the plane's monitor and I stared and stared at the little airplane icon crawling along the great circle route over Cape Breton and Cape Cod, and ordered another glass of wine and leaned back in my chair, trying to keep a lid on my adrenaline.

Over Chicago we hit a lot of turbulence and the plane came teetering in like a toy on a string. *Fucking crash already,* I remember thinking.

After landing we had to wait for an apron bus. Before they built the new international arrivals terminal at O'Hare, you had to transfer from plane to terminal on this contraption that went up and down on hydraulic scissors, dragging the whole thing out interminably. The whole time you just wanted to block it out, just not think about it long enough to catch your breath. But in the controlled environment of an airport your thoughts run along on rails.

As we got off the shuttle and plunged down the hallway to the Customs area, I started to lose my nerve. There was a fire exit, another door leading who-knows-where? You imagined bugging out: jumping a fence, running through a garage, across a tarmac, scaling a fence topped with razor wire.

There was an "amnesty bin" at the end of the hall just before the doors to the terminal, and for a brief moment I considered how I might back my way out of this whole thing: ditch the bag, tell everybody it got confiscated, fade away, leave town. Obviously the amnesty bin is more for disposing quarantined bananas and pot seeds than ditching commercial quantities of pure heroin. Besides, what I really wanted, like a running back who smells endzone, was to pound that bag across the goal line.

Get paid.

On the other side of double steel doors was a room approximately the size of a football field, in fact, the line of scrimmage, Immigration. I scanned the signs on the ceiling to find the correct line, patted the passport, tickets and customs declaration form in my breast pocket, adjusted my tie and tried to look unconcerned. When my turn came I slid the paperwork through the slot and watched breathlessly as an Immigration Agent perused my documents.

"Did you travel anywhere outside Paris?" the agent asked.

"I went to Brussels for the day," I said, stupidly, unnecessarily; Belgium hadn't stamped my book.

The agent stared at the papers for another moment, raised his big stamp and went *stamp-stamp,* and pushed my passport back at me.

At the other end of the terminal was another set of steel doors—simple double doors leading right out to the street, daylight and fresh air strobing through each time someone exited; cabs lined up and waiting, freedom lingering out there.

I hoisted my bag over my shoulder, bypassing the baggage carousels where a cop was walking around with a dog, and headed towards the doors. A single Customs Agent was perched on a stool to the far right, reading a magazine. As I got about a third of the way there, he seemed to stir. I changed direction ever so slightly.

He roused himself. A small group was moving toward him from the right, but he seemed to ignore them.

I looked out the corner of my eyes for someone, anyone I could fall in behind, but everyone seemed blissfully out of reach—and I imagined this is what it must feel like to drown: to take one last desperate look at help swimming strongly away.

Then the agent sauntered ever so slowly out into the middle of the room. My heart raced. Then he looked up. I saw it coming, could *feel* it coming. Oblivious to the rest of the herd, he'd singled me out; and for a second I felt I might just swoon right there. Then some sort of instinct kicked in. I resigned myself to being questioned and headed right at him.

For some seconds he hung back as I did my best to play the part of the unassuming traveler.

"Where are you coming from, sir?" he asked, at an angle.

"Paris," I said.

"Can I see your ticket?"

I handed him my ticket.

"How long were you in Paris?"

"A week."

"What were you doing there?"

"Business."

"What kind of business."

"Magazine. Publishing."

"What magazine?"

And here I faltered. *Nun Civa Orcus. What the fuck was that?* My mind raced for all sorts of explanations. For a second I considered making something up. But that would only mean trouble. You tend to say stupid things when you veer from the script like that. Someone might ask your name, for instance, and under duress you might say Peter Rabbit or Dick Nixon, who the hell knew? Had he detected my hesitation? I had to speak.

"Nun. Civa. Orcus," I said, my voice fluttering like a parakeet to the top of its cage, fluttering back down.

The agent looked me in the eye and seemed to consider for an instant.

"Welcome home," he said. "Have a nice day."

And I walked out the doors into bright sunlight.

Jakarta

Claire and I took a taxi into town, delirious with relief, and joined Barry at the Blackstone Hotel. We were all asleep, sprawled on top of the beds, sweating and exhausted in our travel clothes, when there was a knock on the door. I raised my head, half awake. There was another knock. Claire looked at me, scared. "Hide," she said. "In the closet."

Barry answered the door. A two-hundred-pound African woman in green kaftan and towering orange *gele* sauntered into the room and put a shopping bag down on the bed ... stood there with her back to the room sniffing the air, then turned and walked over to the closet and casually opened the door, sucking her teeth as Claire and I emerged with what little dignity we could muster. Then she took the jackets and left.

The trip was over, we drank champagne, counted money. Claire started jumping up and down on the bed making it "rain," which alarmed me to a great degree. You didn't gloat over your victories, I believed, which only alerted the relevant Gods of mammon, tragedy and comedy for whom the scent of human folly is irresistible, and I scampered around the room collecting bills.

Barry shoved a wad of cash down his pants and hopped across the bed like some great, deranged rabbit, thrusting his hips at Claire, who reciprocated with another shower of fives and tens, twenties, hundreds.

(It became a game with us later, trying to stick the other person with a lot of small notes, which besides being cumbersome evoked unpleasant thoughts about where they'd been. A reechy dollar was about as close as one got to the street.... The money was bundled with elastic bands when it arrived, but we'd take it apart and count it. Stacks were sometimes short. You counted out a thousand dollars and put an elastic around it and threw it in a pile.)

Besides, I was in a hurry to get back home to L and just wanted to be done. The longer one was away, the sketchier the story. I didn't call L on trips. I gave her an itinerary, real or otherwise, and my best guess when I'd be home, and that was it. If we got delayed I made something up. The important thing was to keep it simple. For there are necessary lies one tells, and the gratuitous ones that constitute emotional betrayals. L didn't ask questions about the magazine; I didn't try to make stuff up.

Claire was rolling around the bed with the money now, and Barry was drinking the dregs of a bottle of champagne. I grabbed a stack of twenties and cracked Claire across the ass.

Champagne shot out of Barry's nose.

"Owwww, *asshole!*" Claire bellowed.

"You're crumpling the money," I said.

*

I got back to Northampton by some combination of planes, trains, busses, cabs—memory falters—stashed my briefcase in my study, fought back a paroxysm of conscience and found L doing home-work at the kitchen table.

She looked up, happy to see me. I bent down and kissed her face.

"How come you're working down here? I said.

"I don't know, how come you're an idiot?" she said.

And all was right with the world.

That night we went out to dinner at a fancy Indian restaurant. It was one of those Friday evenings when the lights are coming up in the storefronts and couples are linked arm in arm on the sidewalk.

L was wearing a green, embroidered Afghan vest, these cool high-water wide wale cords and her old cowboy boots. (Funny, memory.) I had on my odd new shoes, a sport coat and a romantic chemise of some sort, no doubt—and a ring L made of square silver wire, which I twirled around the ring finger. We were drink-ing red wine and eating *naan*, and I felt sitting there amongst Smith College faculty and local professionals a sense of ease and of buoyancy, as if by a mere trick of money I had arrived, somewhere anyway....

"We could put up curtains like those in the kitchen," L said, our talk lapsing into easy domesticity.

We were shabby-chic, our apartment consisting of refurbished found objects (my contribution) interspersed with odd treasures: Persian carpets, Colonial silver (hers).

"... or we could leave it open, modern-looking."

"Hmm," she said, not to be outdone in thrift, which is the preeminent virtue among certain New Englanders....

After dinner we walked around Northampton. The first star shone above the Unitarian Church. Dew settled in fields about the town. And in muddy lanes leading down to the river the crickets had begun chanting.

What the hell is wrong with you—I bit my lip, tasting blood—*gadding about the fucking globe when everything you could want is right in front of you?— What do you think you're doing? Who do you think you are?* I chastised myself.

Later that night I closed the door to my study, dialed the combination to my brief case and peered inside. Ten $1,000 bundles were stacked neatly in a corner. I shut the case and locked it; a few hours later opened it again. *So what if I didn't know the first thing about money? Money's not complicated, men's hearts are complicated.*— Or was that the other way around?

Claire called a week or so later. She'd been on the phone with Alhaji. He had a new contract. There were suitcases in Jakarta, Indonesia, $30,000 apiece.

But that wasn't all. Claire thought we could hire out the job of actually carrying. She already had some people in mind: some college kids a friend of hers knew.

If there was ever a time to quit it was now, before one really got started. *Freeze them out; tell them not to call here any more, under any circumstances....*

I wrestled with the idea for an hour, indulging in a pretense of conscience, but there was no getting off now, just as things got interesting.

After objecting to Alhaji's initial suggestion that we take the bags through Abu Dhabi—not wishing to come within mention of the Emirates or the Kingdom or any of those places that generally frown on Western indulgences—we decided on Singapore, and plans were set in motion.

"Cool down Nicky," Alhaji had said to my warm reaction to Abu Dhabi. "I would never let anything happen to you people."

Claire and I met with the new couriers at a local park later that week—recent Bard College grads, barefoot, innocent, sailing a Frisbee. *Oh, hell*, I said under my breath—actually *said* it—feeling exactly like Milton's Satan padding into paradise: *"Ye little think how nigh your change approaches, when all these delights will vanish, and deliver ye to woe."*

In fact they were *not* innocent. No one was innocent. Given half a chance they'd turn out to be perfectly dangerous little children.

Kyle dropped the hippie act in a heartbeat, the long hair and hacky sack left behind in Indonesia. Mary, a rich girl who liked to smoke pot and tool around in a late model Saab, was not so willing to inquire into her own culpability, for anything. Mostly she hung around like a cat waiting to be fed. Jen disappeared down a hole the minute the shit came down; no one seemed to even remember her last name. Anyway, everyone consulted his own conscience, and everyone had her own reasons. They were in, so we called Alhaji and told him that we were ready to go, and a date was set.

Claire and I continued to drink and to plot, immersing ourselves in details, arrivals, departures in order to distract ourselves from the larger meaning of our travels. Think as we might of heroin as a sort of vocation, the province of Burroughses and Baudelaires, Times Square hustlers, jazz players, chanteuses, comedians, "bad lieutenants" and Vietnam Vets—not the healthy, moral middle-class certainly—we knew that we were up to something profoundly wrong. Which was the point, after all....

Once again I told L that I was going to Chicago to work on the magazine. Afraid that I'd be unreachable in Indonesia, I told her that I might be going to Europe to meet with an investor. Which stung, to lie like that—*improbably*, for one; and *serially*. An habitual offender. Because here's the thing: L and I each had our own routines. It was a pattern laid down by august generations preceding us, who managed their companionable and separate lives. And so it was natural that L and I might each have our own bedrooms, bank accounts, bookshelves, cross as we might. And I suspected I was abusing a good will that L extended—that my very life extended to me. Besides, if L had suspected some kind of middling indiscretion she wouldn't have said so anyway, being proud.… Nobody suspects you're smuggling heroin.

Early one morning Claire and I picked the kids up in a rental van and drove to Newark. The three of them sat in the back, Kyle in the middle, tucking his hair behind his ear every five minutes, the girls reserved, feline, not interested in much beyond their immediate personal comfort.

Claire and I never really did "get it." Alhaji wouldn't even want our people to see us, much less know our names and addresses. Ideally, they shouldn't have even known what they were carrying. Problem was, we felt like we owed people an explanation. It was more than a score for us. We simply did not conceive of ourselves as criminals—not in the way professional criminals do, not at first.

Of course we were thoroughly callow. *What had heroin addicts to do with us?* we reasoned—*or their friends or families, or whole societies undermined by a culture of lawlessness to do with us?*

We were merely fulfilling a demand, a prescription. I reckoned myself unaccountable by the same logic everyone reckons himself unaccountable.

In another place and time I might have raised a fist. Or manned the barricades. But in our post-sixties era, cowed by Reagan and Bush Sr. and defeated by a rhetoric so inane that to oppose it would seem stupid, we resorted to punk rock's effete gestures: "Don't know what I want, but I know how to get it."

After returning the van and herding everyone through Newark Airport, we caught a Tower Air flight to Midway in Chicago, spent a night at the Blackstone, then flew Air France to Paris. From Paris we took the train to Brussels and had late dinner at an empty restaurant with deep velour banquets and a smutty waiter who seemed to guess at our secret. The next morning we headed back to the Airport.

It's funny to see people making the same mistakes. Claire was bright, ambitious, seemingly fearless. I plunged into each misadventure, fight, drunk with her the same as I would with any male counterpart. We'd managed to insert ourselves into a managerial position in an international drug ring, recruited couriers, arranged a pick-up, taken care of travel details, paid for everything out of our own pockets, made the leap of imagination. We'd done this behind Alhaji's back. We were standing in line at the Singapore Air terminal in Brussels, when all of a sudden, as if on cue, Piss-Paul came striding through the crowd, scowling, followed by Barry, trotting along as if on a leash. *What the fuck? I thought we'd finished with these jerks after the last trip.*

Claire, unbeknownst to me, had invited Barry. Barry, unbeknownst to Claire, had invited Paul. It didn't add up: four managers, three mules. Everybody was cordial, but I was starting to get that odd-man-out feeling.

It was a long overnight flight from Brussels to Singapore. We all sat separately, the kids meeting furtively by the restrooms all night, Claire drinking red wine, Barry looking nervously over his shoulder at Paul, who sat there scowling.

I worried about Paul for a minute. I had no intention of taking orders, jumping through hoops or anything else. Claire and I had arranged this whole thing, recruited the kids ourselves. No way was Piss-Paul moving in on our trip.

My thoughts went in circles before I finally relaxed and turned my drowsy attention to the flawlessly composed stewardesses floating up and down the aisles in tailored sarongs.

Next morning after breakfast and about an hour before landing the stewardesses came around with boiling hot face towels, which they handed you with metal tongs. I pressed the towel to my face in an intimacy of steam.

The plane landed in Singapore, where we had to debark and get on another plane for Jakarta. The seven of us strolled along half-awake, looking around the airport. As we entered the transit area Claire, Paul and I simultaneously looked back at the luggage scanners. Claire was staring intently at a sign. I took a step closer. "Warning: Death for Drug Traffickers Under Singapore Law." I stood there gaping at the words for long seconds, trying to find some alternate way of construing their meaning. The kids wandered past without noticing.

It was a short flight to Jakarta. We piled into two mildew-smelling cabs and raced into town past matted fields cut with drainage ditches.

Low rain clouds lumbered across distant rice paddies and a dirty brown river followed the highway for some miles before disappearing in a morass, bamboo shacks crowded along the bank on tall pilings sunk into the mud.

Train tracks appeared next to the highway and a human habitation sprang up alongside the track bed. Moldering shacks made from wooden pallets and rusted scraps of corrugated steel, tar paper and cardboard sagged next to smoking trash heaps and standing water. Bent figures moved behind filthy tarps like shadow puppets. Every so often a density of bodies resulted in some kind of industry or other: stripping copper wires or melting rare metals off logic boards—the dismantling and breaking down of wealth, bone by bone, like some great pig…. Then the tracks headed off in another direction carrying with them their unimaginable human cargo, and we headed in ours, briefly chastened.

At an interchange we took a sudden turn up a long, gated drive. A manicured lawn dotted with ornamental trees led to a rambling complex with pitched, shake roofs. We checked into our rooms and met back in the main lobby. An afternoon thunderstorm suffused the room with dark purples and greens, a solid wall of water coming down outside the glass. An hour later the sky was clear.

The kids were out by the pool. Claire and I continued our conversation with Paul and Barry in the tea room, a far corner of the main lobby sectioned off by heavy teak screens with grimacing deities carved into the wood.

We were sitting around a great mahogany table in the shadows. Piss-Paul started in right away. "When we divide up the money from the bags the couriers bring in…."

"Who said we're dividing anything *up*? Those are our recruits," I blurted out, dead silence, just the reverberation of a gamelan dying in the carpet.

Paul scowled. "You mother-fucker," he said, glaring at me for a long second. Then he stormed out, followed by his lapdog, Barry.

I watched them march across the wide marble floor of the lobby and turned to look at Claire.

"Ok, then," she said.

We all met the following morning for a splendid buffet: chafing dishes full of Eggs Benedict, carving station, sushi bar. Every kind of fruit imaginable overflowed a great table in the middle of the dining room, topped by a large, sweating ice sculpture commemorating American Independence Day.

The seven of us were sitting around a table, momentarily reconciled by food, when Paul scowled at me and Claire and said, "You two don't know what the fuck you're doing." Then turning to the kids: "You know the penalty for smuggling drugs into Singapore is *death?*" he said, letting the word *death* hang there.

I stammered something incoherent. We'd told the kids, of course, but Piss-Paul was playing for an effect.

"You two are dangerous because you don't know what you're doing. He's got a fucking stamp from India on his passport. He can't travel with that," Paul said, pointing at Kyle, who tucked a strand of hair behind his ear.

This semblance of fact had Claire and me stumped. We actually took Kyle to the American Consulate later that afternoon to report a lost passport and get a new one. (You didn't want to go back into the States with all kinds of exotic exit and entry stamps on your passport. Better off to keep it simple: Western Europe— to see the Louvre—and home.) Realizing we'd have to do this all over again in Europe to get rid of the Indonesia exit stamps, we scrapped the idea. Paul had panicked us.

"It's not complicated; you take the fucking bags and you go," Paul said, rather disingenuously; he was the one complicating everything—looking through passports, making accusations, finding fault, and generally pissing all over everything.

"Ok, *Paul!* Nobody *knew* about the *death penalty* until we saw the signs in the airport," I said as savagely as I could under the circumstances. "We're not making anyone do anything they don't want to do."

But this was so much backpedaling. Paul walked out of the dining room with a flourish, Barry at his heels. I sat there staring at the ice sculpture. I could never quite make those things out. Beautiful red and orange fruits ringed the ice—off limits because they're grown in human shit, the guidebook said.

The next morning we called Alhaji, who remained opaque, a name, a voice on the telephone. I hadn't even met him yet. Alhaji gave us the telephone number of the hotel our connection was staying in. No one answered, so I took a cab downtown.

Cars moved in and out of lanes like flights of birds. Busses bounded through traffic with passengers clinging to the roof. Mopeds and small-stroke motorcycles weaved in and out with riders in dust masks and bandanas. Above it all, along *Jalan Thamrin*, Jakarta's main boulevard, cycloptic office towers confusedly turned one way and another like drunken conventioneers with corporate nametags.

We took a side street and turned into a lane with trash-filled puddles. The hotel was down an alley, a series of rooms off a courtyard. I got out of the cab and went into a tiny open-aired office with a radio bleating Indonesian pop music. No one answered the bell. Behind the desk was a dry-erase board with guest names. The two Filipinos staying in the last room seemed likely candidates. I knocked nicely on their door, then rapped hard, shaking the flimsy material. There was a stirring inside. The door accordionned open revealing a hungover-looking individual in undershorts, perplexed, shocked, affronted that somebody had been banging on his door so early.

"Do you know Alhaji?" I asked. He just looked at me. "Do you know Alhaji? I asked again, and again he gave no answer. "Look, I'm with Alhaji. Give me the bag. The bag."

There was a flicker of comprehension and he stepped back into the room. Another fellow was lying on a mattress on the floor, squinting at the light. The first guy picked up a black leather bag out of the corner and held it against his chest. I took a step into the room and put my hand on the bag. He flinched slightly, and I took hold of it. He gripped the bag tight for an instant, but as I pulled it toward me he slowly loosened his grasp. I took the bag and stepped back through the door, looked back at him an instant, turned and left.

In the cab I held the bag in my lap. There was a perfect little dime-sized hole cut in the leather, a piece of electrical tape over the hole—which kind of bummed me out. We were talking millions of dollars of heroin. I didn't really know how precisely the stuff was weighed or the chain of custody, but it seemed to me you'd be in a whole lot of trouble if they got the idea you were stealing product.

Along the road back to the hotel I stared out the window of the cab at a series of monuments that seemed to tell a story: the official government version of events leading to the brutal elimination of Communists in 1965. This was still very much Suharto's Indonesia, the little stencil-image of him in felt *peci* graffitied on walls and abutments just a quaint reminder that Indonesia was a country ruled by a strong-man.

Back at the hotel Claire came at me in a panic. The kids were gone. Piss-Paul had taken off with them to Jogjakarta, a resort town three hours away. He'd turned them against us, stolen them, which could mean any number of things. At best we were faced with having to carry the bags ourselves. At worst, who knew?

Under the circumstances it seemed like a good idea to get out of the hotel, so we packed our bags and walked straight through the lobby to a waiting taxi cab. In town we registered under fake names at a swank Arab high-rise, a jagged piece of black glass thrust into the sky, locked the kid's passports in the hotel's safety deposit box and took a suite high up in bright sunlight.

Claire looked like she was going to cry. We ordered a pot of black coffee and a bottle and settled down in our war room. Then we beat our brains out trying to decide what to do next.

You hold a problem up to the light and turn it around, convinced there's some facet you haven't considered, some solution you've overlooked. Problem was, we'd failed to work through our position, were *en prise,* as they say in chess. What if Paul told Alhaji what we were up to? What if he told the cops? We were *pinned,* in fact, a bag of heroin in our lap.

In addition to the immediate problem was a finer existential point, which escaped me at the moment, though I think Claire was acutely aware of it:

"If we fuck this up, we're right back in Northampton asking for our jobs back at *Spoleto*."

"You think they'd have us?"

"Probably not."

"It wouldn't be that bad," I said, attempting *cavalier*.

"Oh no?"

"Nah— *Hey Claire, you got that deuce on table 10?*" I said.

"No," she said, exhaling a plume of cigarette smoke into the artificial air.

"You know the specials?"

"No."

"You've got food up."

"Ok, shut the hell up...."

We'd been talking in circles and came back once again to the crux:

"So, we've got the bags, they have to come to us."

"Or tell Alhaji what we're up to...."

"Unless we tell him first."

I plunked an ice cube into each tumbler and poured in scotch.

There was no way around it; the only thing to do was fess up to Alhaji. (Sacrifice the knight.) Then at least Piss-Paul wouldn't have anything on us.

"I hope he's okay with it."

"If he's not okay, you take the call."

No, you take it.

Sunlight pierced the blinds as call to prayer echoed from loud-speakers across the city. I looked up at plastic arrows in the corner of the room pointing to Mecca, abandoned a fleeting impulse to move them around. My head was killing me. Claire dialed the phone. Dialed again. Dialed a third time. A small voice came over the earpiece. Claire waited and waited. Then another, cautious voice came on.

"Hello?"

"Alhaji, it's Claire. How are you, Sir?"

"I am fine; how are you?"

"Well, we have a problem with Paul…."

Claire laid the whole thing out.

At first I couldn't understand what Alhaji was saying. Then I was able to make it out, part through the phone's earpiece, part by osmosis.

"I am very happy. I have been looking for somebody to take initiative. You tell Doctor and his brother (code for Paul and Barry) to call me. Let me talk to Nicky"

Claire handed me the phone.

"Hello, Alhaji?"

"Yes, how are you?"

"I'm fine, thanks…."

We called the old hotel, but there was no answer, so we killed some time. I took a walk through *Pasar Baru*, a vibrant marketplace along a dirty canal. Apparently the Dutch had thought to create a new Amsterdam in the tropics, creating instead a stagnant, malarial waterway.

A crowd of Chinese tourists were taking photographs on the sidewalk. A cabbie smoked a fragrant Djarum in the shadow of an arch. And an old man in straw hat plied the banks of the canal with a toy rod and orange bobber for the few carp that bumped among trash and lotus flowers.

You went over a bridge festooned with flags and a pagoda. The better shops were along the sidewalk.

In Kamal's Tailor Shop, Mr. Kamal greeted me personally and led me over to a book filled with fabrics. "These are the latest designer textiles from Europe," he said, flipping through the swatches. We went over to a wall and Kamal slid out a bolt of tropical wool in olive green and draped the end over my shoulder.

Then Kamal's assistant began making an extensive set of measurements: around the chest, across the back, down the back, the arm, etc. We decided on an Italian-style suit, trim, single-breasted, two buttons, two vents, and he began to cut a pattern. The next day the suit was basted together. After some tugging this way and that they were ready to finish.

I went back a day later for the final product: narrow shoulders, low rise, slight flair in the trousers, a somewhat Asian interpretation of the Italian. Bruce Lee circa 1968, very groovy.

Finally we got word that Piss-Paul and Lapdog Barry had come back from Jogjakarta and were at a small hotel nearby with the kids. I changed into my suit, a pale violet dress shirt and new shoes, and we pulled up in a cab and took a small elevator smelling of machine oil to the top, sixth floor of the hotel and rapped on the door. Paul was out.

"Call Alhaji," Claire said to Barry, who cringed. "Where are the kids?"

We moved in next door. The kids were a little sourpussed at first. Kyle and Mary moped around at the far side of the pool. Then they realized it was back to business and they got very cordial.

Paul and Barry flew out a couple days before us as Alhaji had instructed them to do. I gave them each a bag, though that left us short one. Claire wasn't happy about it, but I figured it was the price of doing business. Next morning they called to let us know they were okay in Brussels. That was the last we'd have to do with them.

All of a sudden the kids didn't seem so solid. Kyle was sitting on the floor in the hallway sniffling, hacky sack at his side.

"What's going on?" I said.

"Nothing," he said peevishly, tucking a strand of hair behind his ear. He was still a kid, angry at that world; had I paid attention I might have recognized in him a semblance of myself.

I knocked on the door to their room. Jen and Mary were lounging on the bed in their underwear. Mary was a blonde-haired beauty, her blue eyes hollowed out from drugs. Jen looked like she wanted to fight. I think they regarded me as some kind of yuppie simply because I was 30. Claire had alluded to Kyle's father being some kind of 60s radical.

"I'm going out, do you guys need anything?" I said.

They simply said No.

Then Claire came in the room and started messing around on the bed. Despite her talent for picking out a dyke, I think she was barking up the wrong tree.

Kyle and Mary were together, with Jen grafted on in some ornamental fashion. Mostly I think they tormented one another, and whomever they lured into their fly paper, nothing more than that.

Fuck this. I walked out of the room, past Kyle in the hallway and out to the clubs to get rousing drunk.

The next morning we rifled the kids' stuff, confiscated a box of Xanax (sold over the counter in Indonesia), took Kyle's hacky-sack, which he was always drawing attention to himself with, and got everyone haircuts.

Kyle was in the barber's chair looking earnestly into the mirror. "Regular cut," I said to the barber. Kyle groped for words. "Regular cut," I repeated.

The girls were peeking around the corner, giggling. Lots of hair accumulated on the floor. Kyle looked in the mirror with a serious expression. He seemed changed. Mary rubbed against him like a cat.

Now we could concentrate on Singapore. Though common sense dictated staying as far away from the bags as possible, Claire and I decided we should go as a group to give moral support to the couriers. We were all just American tourists in Indonesia flying back to Europe to continue our vacation.

The kids insisted they were ready to go, unfazed by the alleged death penalty. In fact, we were of the unanimous opinion, rightly or wrongly, that we could bribe our way out, that Alhaji would pull strings, that if it came to it the American government would intervene long before any heads rolled, that we were all safe and always would be safe.

The flight out of Indonesia was uneventful. We gingerly exited the plane in Singapore, went through passport control and headed down a wide, empty hallway as early morning light streaked through high windows. A moving walkway conveyed us toward the end of the terminal where two bored-looking guards milled about, a few hundred yards away. Just as we seemed to attract their notice, a loud, dull thud like a fastball thudding into a catcher's mitt echoed through the terminal. Kyle's bag was sitting on the walkway. Claire's eyes widened. The strap on Kyle's bag had broken under the strain.

The bags were sleek, leather garment bags, but they didn't open up like regular garment bags; they just had zippered pockets on either side. In the middle was a two-inch thick slab of heroin, bulging somewhat obscenely in the middle and shrink-wrapped in carbon to create a false bottom image, supposedly. (Claire said the bags were supposed to have red pepper, to throw off scent dogs, which struck me as so much b.s. being passed along.)

The bag was supported by a steel rod, (also with heroin inside—no wasted space here); leather loops riveted to the bag attached to the shoulder strap by a metal ring. One of the leather loops had ripped under the strain. The bags were heavy, 10 kilos of heroin in each.

Without missing a beat Kyle tied the loose end of the shoulder strap onto the center handle and hoisted it back over his shoulder. In front of us was an x-ray machine the size of a bus. The girls stepped into line first, followed by Claire, then Kyle and me. The bags were so heavy that the girls needed all their strength to lift them onto the conveyor belt, and I wondered if I had the nerve to fake a heart attack if there was a problem.

We headed through the metal detector and waited nervously, glancing back at the x-ray screen. We'd put as much stuff as we could into the pockets to create clutter.

The agent froze an image to look more closely. Shoes, hangers. What was he looking at? My mind raced, an initial adrenaline spike coursing into my brain with thoughts of *Run. Kill. Relax. Relax.* It was like focusing binoculars. Then the agent hit a button and the conveyor spit our luggage out.

"Let's go," Claire said to Mary and Jen, who looked down at the bags like they wanted nothing to do with them. After gathering everything up we waited in a little glassed-in departure lounge right next to the x-ray, dreading the thought each time the door opened that it was the cops rushing in. Finally they called our flight and we barged onto the plane, impatient for takeoff.

It was a long flight back to Europe. We spent the night separately, dozing, drinking, listening to music, trying to stave off laxity. We breezed through Belgian customs and checked into a new hotel under newly made-up aliases, not the usual ones, careful to stay away from Piss-Paul and Lapdog Barry, lest they have some kind of mischief in mind again.

We sent Kyle, all GQ, to the American Embassy in Brussels to report a lost passport. In an hour he had a brand new book in his hand. No stamps from Indonesia or India. In Paris Mary and

Jen did the same, wandering out of the hotel and wandering back as casually as a couple of house cats.

The rest of the trip was anti-climactic. Chicago was a breeze. "You take the bags and you go." Piss-Paul was right.

We called Alhaji when we got into town.

"I am very happy for you people." he said. "You will have to come to Africa, Nicky."

Then he called his connections who came to the hotel to pick up the bags and leave money. Since this was a large delivery, it took a couple pick-ups to hand over the bags and a couple extra drop-offs of money. After each transaction we changed hotels and called Alhaji with a new telephone number. Different Africans showed up. (Alhaji, we found out later, kept Paul and Barry cooped up for over a week, waiting to get paid in full.)

Finally it was all done, the money divided up, and we went out to dinner at an Italian restaurant on the North Side, an old bank with marble floors and heavy oak tables. I was drinking grappa the whole time, Tumi bag with $30,000 at my side. The girls were all made up. Kyle was dressed in this beautiful new white linen shirt, pomade in his hair. At some point alcohol loosened tongues and whatever little residual bad feeling there was came out. They'd ditched us in the middle of a trip.

"You ever pull that shit again," I said to Kyle.

His head jerked up.

Claire was shaking her head, *No, no.*

Kyle said something back. He was a sassy kid.

And as I reached for my drink I knocked a goblet of red wine right into his lap. "Ah, man, I'm sorry," I said, though I wasn't.

Beginner's Luck

Upon return to Western Mass. I packed the Northampton house into a moving van and drove to the Cape. L was waiting in a summer rental out on Pilgrim Heights.—

The great migration, that deep pattern of our lives, from that first college summer I turned twenty....

On 6A I turned up a moonlit sand drive into some dunes, unlocked a cottage door and slid in next to L in sea-dampened linen, some kind of Black Sam Bellamy come for his Goody Hallett.

In the morning I drank coffee on the front steps watching gulls drift over the dunes to the bay, the silver cottages lining the road like little fish, and daydreamed of a vague, future happiness—sitting in this same place thirty, forty years hence, having made it to old age, the work done, heartache ameliorated, regrets forgotten....

L came onto the porch. "You're leaving again?"

"I have to. The magazine."

"How long?"

"Same as last time."

"I'm leaving in August, you know." L was going back to finish school.

"I won't be long."

There were two more bags to be picked up. It seemed that Claire and I had fortuitous timing, heroin arriving freely, so I hustled down to Jakarta again with two new guys, Zane and Brad.

Brad was 130 pounds and could belt out Amazing Grace like Patti LaBelle. We'd shared a house my second year in grad. school, a harsh New Hampshire winter of celebratory drinking, bright cold Sunday mornings and dead furnaces. Brad's car broke down on the center strip of Rt. 95 in Kittery in a river of slush, and Brad, in women's Fleuvogs, finally called it quits. He'd been living in Chicago and didn't have a lot going on. His band had broken up. He was temping and single. He was perfect for the job; but what I mean to say is he was also my friend, or had been my friend—I wasn't entirely sure—and I felt, recruiting him, like some kind of lethal jellyfish drifting into his path, unable to help either of us.

Claire recruited Zane, whose red hair and deep-set eyes lent him a vaguely sinister appearance, like he had an uncle somewhere running guns for the IRA. Zane was ubiquitous, basically. I'd seen this guy at house parties in Provincetown. I'd worked with him at a restaurant in Northampton. We had mutual Boston friends. Another social butterfly with no pressing engagements, he could drop everything at a moment's notice and be gone for weeks on end, and there was no end of the referrals of eager, amoral young men willing to risk anything and everything for a new wardrobe.

Somehow, being in Jakarta again was stranger than the first time. The second time was the un-romanticized version. This time we were going to need more than beginner's luck.

I've thought a lot about beginner's luck. This story is about beginner's luck, which is just the doing of a thing without asking oneself how or why, because there is no how or why, and for a moment there was something almost pure about it all, if you can believe that.

Things were all fucked up from the start. There were no Singapore Air flights out of Brussels or Paris. We finally managed to get seats out of Zurich from an agency that bought up blocks of tickets and headed to Switzerland on a lovely train ride through alpine foothills. The train, more of a sightseer than an express, rocked us half-asleep. Then the cops came on the train out of nowhere and eyed me a good deal for some reason. Sometimes it seems everyone can see something you can't.

After checking into Hotel Rathaus in Old Town, we wandered the hills above Zurich window-shopping and eating *raclette*—melted cheese and potatoes—and finally made our way to the shore of *Zurichsee,* the lake pinioned beneath a sharp blue sky, long, steady, cool stream of air blowing down from the Alps, depressed to find ourselves amidst this productive and orderly Swiss-German society doing a kind of existential walk-of-shame.

That's partly true. I was happy to be free of Claire's incessant conspiracy-mongering and jockeying for position, enjoying a moment with the fellows. Zane carried a bottle of wine under his jacket as we strolled back into town on cobbled streets looking up at church spires and sunlight shifting in the trees.

"Oh my God," Brad said, overwhelmed by the storybook setting.

"Take it easy Brad," said Zane, an inveterate wise-ass. "Have a drink."

Brad drank and passed the bottle.

"So where can we get some McDonald's around here?" Zane said, tilting the bottle back....

The next day they took off in search of some kind of scene they'd read about in *The Big Gay Travel Guide to Europe* and I wandered the town alone. Up a steep flight of granite stairs near the University, in a tiny park looking out through the trees, two old men were playing giant chess. The fellow playing black lugged his queen's knight out, while the white player stood at a little distance, hands clasped behind his back. I watched from a stone bench on the sideline, possessed of a momentary sense of well-being, a tiny figure crouching in the corner of a Chinese landscape painting, safely hidden amid the great cosmic hubbub.

White dragged his bishop out, pinning the knight.

"Que bueno," the black player chuckled, the game developing along known lines until somebody improvised, or blundered, or simply wandered out beyond his depth.

I walked back down the stairs, crossed the Limmat and found a restaurant just opening for dinner. On the second floor, in a bare stucco room with long wooden tables and straight-backed chairs, I poured from a carafe of white wine and waited for the fondue to arrive, watching summer light reflected off the off the buildings across the river.

That night I happened upon a piano bar. They were singing in German. I stayed on, moving my lips and drinking kirschwasser; at midnight stumbled back to the hotel past prostitutes loitering outside hostess bars. *"Schwanzlutscher,"* hissed an old platinum blonde in patent leather knee boots, appraising my lack of interest.

Brian and Zane were lying in their beds, smoking in the dark when I got back to the room. *"Gute nacht schwanzlutscher,"* I said, laughing; and in the morning we caught our flight to Indonesia.

*

The first night in Jakarta I called Alhaji from a comfortably seedy hotel room with a big leather chair, a desk and a bar. Alhaji instructed me to find one *Aukie Wierma,* a lost courier belonging to "the other people," as Alhaji referred to his associates. (Just how the pieces fit together I never figured out.) So, I found a phone book and started calling hotels in alphabetical order. "Do you have an Aukie Wierma there? Wierma. Wierma. Aukie. W-i-e-r-m-a.... No? Ok, thanks." Etc. Finally, after about an hour of this, some front desk clerk said, *Yes,* so I called Alhaji and gave him the phone number. No explanation was given. There never seemed to be an explanation.

Free for now, I headed out into the warm evening air, hailed a Datsun B-210 deathtrap reeking of gasoline, jerry-rigged gas tank wedged in the space behind the back seat, and went speeding the length of *Jalan Thamrin,* the night full of neon and chlorophyll and fumes—dimly aware of the world dropping like a coin through a hole in the floor.

You know that feeling of standing outside time? That's what crime is like; it's actually quite lovely for an initial moment you can't seem to recapture, like so many first things, and then in the long run it's just lonely, and then it's terrifying, but at first you are taken in by the illusion of an adventure.

In fact, no one knew where I was.

Not my parents. Not L. The only people I loved in the world. Nobody.

You learned to lie. You lied to protect others as well as yourself. Yet each time you lied you felt a stab of remorse. So you lied all the better....

Later we stuffed the bags of heroin into a closet and went out drinking. What the hell? No one knew who we were, and we weren't going to brood over the damn things

Our favorite club was "Top Ten," a skeevy little dive with aspiring Japanese gangsters and underage Indonesian prostitutes who did some kind of fashion show in the middle of the dance floor at midnight. I was drinking warm 32-ounce *Bintang* beers, the national beverage, it seemed. The music sucked. That fucking Whitney Houston song played every hour. They seemed to like Michael Jackson a lot, too, or thought we did.

Zane went up to the deejay booth to make a request. The deejay cued a record. Zane walked back to the table head thrown back in laughter as "Thriller" came on again full blast.

I was skulking out of the bathroom, that point in the evening when you have to take that first big piss and you zip up and the face in the mirror is grinning at you—the kind of face you'd like to take a swing at—and tripped over something behind the door. A bucket of vomit sloshed back and forth. Then the water roiled.

As we left the bar at the end of the night, Mamasan was in the doorway hawking her girls.

"Good, this one. You like take home?" she said.

From a distance they looked grown up. Up close you understood they were fourteen.

The next day was equatorially hot and humid, like peering through fogged glass. On the way to the bank to change money I stopped at one of the roadside *guarangs*—pushcart, kerosene cook fire, wok—ordered chicken satay and ate squatting on a grassy shoulder gazing at tall glass buildings and banyan trees drifting through yellow smog. I looked down, confused for an instant. The cook was casually washing her wok out in the gutter. In a couple of days that acid reflux taste of giardia would start.

We needed to change several thousand dollars, which I'd stashed in my front pockets, into *rupiah*. We needed cash in the likely event we had to change our return date. This part of the job required a little finesse. Try to fly without round-trip tickets, try to buy your ticket the day of travel, try to change your ticket too many times—try using cash in general—and you risked alerting the Passenger Analysis Unit, which even before 9-11 was busy compiling "watch lists."

They acted put upon at the bank, and I was starting to get a little nervous. Who knew what a phone call to the cops could mean? As a matter of fact, we'd smuggled cash into the country without making a proper declaration.

I headed back to the hotel, wary of all the little pilot fish waiting outside hotels and banks and just about everywhere else. Some of these were perfectly harmless types offering little symbiotic services; others had a keen eye out for fellows like me, ready to tip off the cops or local gangsters. This reality bred a reasonable paranoia, and on the way back to the hotel, valets, shoe shines, hawkers of cigarettes and any number of older fellows sitting aimlessly in lobbies seemed to multiply by three, discouraging any desire to loiter. The trick was to keep moving, to always look as if one had a destination.

I got in the elevator and punched all the buttons. Later that day I insisted on changing cabs, twice. (It's true, the concierge recorded your destination.) I was starting to lose it.

Brad left for the airport first, skulking out to a cab like a drag queen in high heels. The next day Zane and I left. First we killed time in the lobby of the President Hotel, a big dowdy room occupied by old Indonesian men taking afternoon tea in the yellow sunlight that filtered through tall windows. We were playing a game of hearts or something. Zane's red hair stood out like a red flag. A Good Samaritan warned us about playing cards in public. Against *Sharia*.

At the airport ticket counter they informed us of a tax of about twenty dollars on each ticket. We'd spent all of our money. There was just enough for the tickets. No tax. Nor did they accept credit cards or have a bank machine. This was a problem. We sat on a bench to confer. A well-dressed Indonesian businessman checked his watch. I accosted him without thinking twice. *We had a plane to catch, had miscalculated. Could he help us?* The man handed over the money, dismissing my attempt to get his address to pay him back with a wave of his hand.

Then, as we were paying for our ticket, they tried to make Zane check one of his bags. It was like he had a sign on his back; the mere sight of his red hair seemed to rouse every minor functionary from his official slumbers into a zealous burst of activity.

Zane had two bags: a fake garment bag and a duffel bag. One you could hang in a little closet inside the front door of the plane; the other you carried on.

He glanced at me. I shook my head. The hard and fast rule was that you took your bags onto the plane with you, avoiding whatever monkey-business goes on with the checked luggage.

"I need to carry my bags on," Zane said.

"We have a single carry-on limit," the Singapore Air agent said.

"Look, we have some very expensive cameras, and we're not stowing them under the plane," I said.

"Sir...."

"Let me speak to the supervisor, please," I said.

The plane landed in Singapore. We went through the big x-ray machine and boarded a jumbo jet for a night flight to Europe. The plane rose to thirty thousand feet and roared into the night, a vast darkness, lit here and there by little points of light below.

When the fasten seatbelt light went off and the no smoking light went off, I walked to the back for a smoke. Unable to sleep, I spent the next couple hours hanging around the spacious aft section of the big A380, smoking and eavesdropping on conversations. Men in sports jackets and beards murmured happily in their languages. I leaned against the bulkhead, forehead pressed to the cold glass, and contemplated the Arabian Desert below—washed down a Valium with a double gin and tonic, found an open row of seats to lie down in and wrapped myself in a blanket, intent on sleeping to Europe.

Somewhere in the middle of the night I woke with a start. Some bodily presence, or *prescience,* had jolted me wide-awake. *Oh, Jesus,* I groaned aloud, a preemptive baby-shit hot in my drawers, my gut issuing orders: "Everything get out, get out now!" And I was on my feet and mincing my way to the back of the plane thinking, *Please, God, don't let there be a line.*

Happily, airplane bathrooms are compact, allowing for multitasking. A kind of heavy weather seamanship. Up on the deck to tie the tiller over, down in the galley to retch.

I exited the bathroom breathing hard. An hour later I woke up again, and every hour on the hour for the next eight hours my stomach ejected a thin gruel of bilge water and *Scallops Singapore Air.* At first light I made a formal protest to a stewardess who produced a charcoal tablet with ill-concealed contempt.

In Brussels we met up with Claire. I crashed for a couple hours. Later that afternoon they woke me. Time to move, but the thought of riding a train in my state was intolerable, so I decided to head back and let Claire shepherd Brad and Zane with their high heels and red hair the rest of the way home.

Everything was booked solid, except for a first class ticket to New York. I still remember that seat. A seat like that you lay back in like a Roman Emperor. Half expecting someone's elbow in my ribs, or foot in my derriere, I accepted the obligatory glass of champagne, smirked knowingly at my fellows in first class and passed out.

Later, I caught a commuter to Boston, then took a little Provincetown-Boston Airways Cessna to the Cape.

In the gloaming the plane bumped across the water and the outer Cape came into view. As we descended a little filament flickering inside a green thunderhead interposed itself in the middle distance and the pilot banked the plane. By the time we came three-sixty the storm had passed, and when the plane set down and we got off, the dunes were damp and clean and smelled of rosehips and salt and sweet fern, and I was home and never, ever wanted to leave again.

Alhaji

A month later we were in Europe again. Alhaji said he wanted to
see us, so Claire and I hightailed it to the Beninese Consulate in
Paris to get visas, then to Hospital Pasteur to get our *Cartes Jaune*
before flying to Togo.

In a sense, all airports are alike. We arrived in Lomé early in
the morning and ordered coffee at a little shop off the main con-
course. Then we sat and stared onto the tarmac like sunbathers at
seaside. Pale sunlight streaked the terrazzo floor. A few janitors
made their rounds, emptying out wastebaskets and sweeping up
peanut shells. Soon passengers began to trickle in, and the terminal
was crowded with every kind of traveler. Businessmen with elegant
leather satchels and émigrés with luggage fashioned from cardboard, packing tape and twine all maneuvered in the mid-morning
heat.

Claire and I bluffed our way into a first class lounge and slept for an hour. Then we boarded an Air Afrique plane for the short flight to Benin. As we got closer I wondered more intently about this person we called Alhaji. No one seemed to know his actual name. (If they did, they didn't speak it.) Or how many people he controlled. Or who controlled him. Or if he'd ever even *made* a *haj*.

We telephoned from the airport and Alhaji's secretary, Binga, a short efficient fellow in a pez, met us curbside in a Range Rover and drove us a short distance to a residential neighborhood, gated concrete houses hidden from the hot, dusty road.

Binga honked the horn and somebody hurried out of the shade and swung open a corrugated steel gate to a compound. Several fellows were washing a small fleet of cars. Binga showed us through the front door of the house to a cool, dim interior. Alhaji shouted a greeting as he came down the stairs. I heard him before I saw him. Then he came around the corner, tall, easy-going, dressed in beige linen trousers and band-collar shirt. Broad, sympathetic face not yet beginning to slacken. Forty-five, perhaps, in the fullness of his strength.

"Ah, Claire, you have put on some fat," he said admiringly, slapping at his neck. "Like pig! How do you like Africa, Nicky?"

"I like it," I said.

The domestic staff came in and knelt before us, and lunch was served.

Alhaji talked on and on. He ate little, afflicted by indigestion. A lot of what he said alluded to people I didn't know. In all it was a little hard to follow.

Later we went for a drive in the Mercedes coupe, top down, Shabba Ranks blaring on the radio, the car jolting in and out of traffic past pedestrians and mopeds, this charismatic Nigerian drug dealer at the wheel laughing his head off. We'd just made him millions.

If it were any other venture I would have said, *OK, we did it. What's next?* But there was a mystery at the end of this, pulling strings. Who was this person? How real was his power? And what was my proximity to that power?

Avenues of association crisscrossed interminably here in Benin. Alhaji was rumored to be President Soglo's Security Chief. He claimed to own several businesses: import-export, car dealership, cotton ginnery. And he seemed familiar with any number of expats, cabinet ministers and local gangsters. As I watched him taking phone calls that seemed to relate to at least half a dozen different intrigues, of which we were just one, it occurred to me that his genius lay in the ability to keep a whole bunch of things going at once—*that* a matter of seeing the essential outlines of things to where his self interest lay. He had an ability to simplify.

Contrary to that urge (or perhaps it merely facilitated his calculation of self-interest) he kept us somewhat mystified about the way things worked, all the while holding out a promise of riches.

"I want you people to know, I would never let anything happen to you. I am like an eagle," he said, standing and spreading his arms wide at lunch, "and I will keep you under my...." he struggled for the word *wings*. "I would never force you to sign a contract. Maybe you will sign a contract. If you manage to escape with your life, perhaps you will realize one million, one point two million in one year's time. I want you people to know, I would never let anything happen to you."

If you ever doubted Alhaji, next minute he'd do something to win you over. That evening he grilled fish on a charcoal fire behind the house, and we ate "African style," Alhaji, Claire and I squatting against a cement wall in the dark, grabbing the hot, flaky fish off the coals with our bare hands.

Afterwards we went out in Cotonou, like most West African cities darkness punctuated by bare light bulbs and shadows. There was a busy club on the outskirts of town, the parking lot crowded with expensive cars. It must have been 99 degrees when we went through the front door, and every ten feet inside seemed to get ten degrees hotter. Claire looked miserable in a wool dress she'd worn on the plane trip from Europe, and I was seized by a malicious impulse.

"Let's dance," I said.

Claire looked at me with loathing. Alhaji was looking around, so I went on the dance floor by myself. There were just a couple other people dancing to that ubiquitous "High Life" sound. Then the music changed to rhythm and blues, then to some kind of old 50s rock and roll. The dance floor was suddenly crowded, sweeping everyone up in the rhythm, the dancers like a single animal pulsing beneath the skin of music…. *Let me remember this*, I thought hard, and not for the first time in my travels. *Let me remember this moment, even if the worst thing happened, let me remember this moment and let it save me.*

Alhaji was out there dancing with me now, pleased at my pleasure in his Africa. Then Claire was out there looking frumpy and pissed off. *Fuck her; how many lesbian bars in Northampton had I been forced to hang around in?*

At some point we made our way to the back of the club and I was standing there holding a drink, looking around when Claire elbowed me in the ribs. "Go, now," she mouthed. "We need to leave right now. Go to the door. Fast."

There must be some people after us, I thought, and without looking around started moving towards the door as quickly as possible without attracting attention. We got through the crowd and into the car and we were merging into a short line of cars when several men came out the front door at a jog. They were on us in an instant, one man at Alhaji's open passenger window, another striding toward my door with his hand thrust out.

"Don't let them see your face," Alhaji said as we flattened ourselves against the back seat. Then a big grinning face appeared in the window and a man reached into the car and shook my hand and slipped me a business card. "Adetosoye, import/export," it read. "Give me a call," the bearer said. I turned to look at Alhaji who was having a somewhat pained conversation with the fellow in front.

"Ok, see you," Alhaji said and pulled out into traffic. Discretion prevented us from asking who they were, though it was clear enough they were some kind of rival "Alhajis."

Next day we went to see a witch doctor, which we did whenever we visited. I think Alhaji did this partly because he believed in it— as a heroin smuggler you had to believe in some guiding force that could be petitioned or bribed—and partly as a means to instill loyalty in us. We thought of it as a field trip.

I took off my shoes and Claire covered her head as we went through a dilapidated church to an inner courtyard where this fat woman sat atop a pile of rubble with a goat.

We were each given the stub of a candle into which we were supposed to whisper questions we wanted answered. The marabout would answer. The money we gave would go toward slaughter of the goat, the goat's blood to be mixed with oatcakes and used to feed the poor, who would be instructed to say prayers for our safe travel.

Okay, fine; if it involved feeding the needy, it seemed reasonable. I whispered into the candle and looked up at the old woman, who looked back at me blankly as she began to speak. "You must remain faithful and you will never encounter any problems," she said through Alhaji; and I wondered how much he was adding. "You need to be careful of your health, you need to avoid drinking and smoking or you could have a problem with your leg. Don't eat papa ... papaya. One day you will be king of the country."

The last part sounded entirely like Alhaji; and so it must have been Alhaji, consciously or not, trying simultaneously to shape an image of himself, after which he sought to shape us.

I admit it: I was taken by the allure of money and power and danger. I discretely copied little gestures: the way Alhaji would carry his telephone around the house, a phrase or two, a style of driving and dressing. But all that was just posturing, of course.

The fact is I began to feel as if I were participating in the history of my time, and though history crushes men, it also singles them out and bears them aloft for an instant before dashing them under the wheels. I had business in Africa and Europe and Chicago—the buying and selling of a commodity. The filling of a demand. No pretense of virtue. Nor theft of public ideals.

Should I say what I really thought?

No. I belonged to no one. I was out on my own now.

SQUiD

Along the way I started a little Magazine (and by a sleight of hand substituted *Squid* magazine for *Nun Civa Orcus* so that my European trips were now in the service of my own work, as far as anyone was concerned.)

The year was 1994. Bill Clinton was in office. Baseball was on strike. And The New York Times Business Day ran an article: "The American Economy, Back on Top."

Squid was a love letter to Provincetown, a fishing village at the end of Cape Cod, a raucous, amoral place of stark, beautiful light. Home to fishermen and artists and drag queens, it offered a clue how one might live by one's wits. You came here to test yourself, and you either had a little success or a little fun or a little smash-up.

My friend Peter and I plotted *Squid* in secret over a dozen late winter nights. Pete had come rocketing back to earth somewhere over the dunes in North Truro after a spectacular flame-out at Hampshire and tilted into Provincetown with the bearing of William Howard Taft and Ignatius J. Reilly, black hair, baby-face and wire-rimmed spectacles.

We'd worked together at *Café Blasé,* a little outdoor place all pastel lanterns and geraniums, remarkable for attracting like-talented individuals and binding them together.

Those were summers of prodigious drinking; friends made and lost; fortunes squandered—though not really.

(There were still ways to outwit the 20th century. You could smoke pot back in the kitchen and bullshit your way through your shift, declare nothing, spend your days biking through the dunes, drinking coffee, reading, pretending to write novels; scrape mussels off the breakwater or beg culls off lobstermen on the pier, attire oneself in thrift store finery, go out dancing, drink wine all night, find the occasional obliging waitress and stiff the landlord on your last month's rent so he couldn't beat you out of the security….)

Then all at once it was over and everyone filed out of town as after a dance or funeral: shades drawn, shops closed, shingles taken in and stored in basements.

A couple hundred souls hung on like oak leaves, craving the solitude of an abandoned summer town, or just not smart enough to leave; I didn't know which. I needed to be alone, so I rented an unfurnished three-story apartment on the top of Conant Street that let a long draft under the front door and up the stairs, whistling to be let out. From the third floor bedroom I looked out over the harbor, king of nothing—unanimous in thought and deed….

L was back in Northampton finishing up school. I'd driven her back and helped her get set up in an apartment. If I was a lousy emotional partner, I was an energetic house mover at any rate….

Peter lived a couple blocks over. One night I trudged through the snow and wind and blackness to see what was up.

Peter had a bottle of Jagermeister. That's the short version of how the magazine got started.

Essentially it was bluster. Having talked for months about starting a magazine, I felt obliged to actually do it. (How fortunate to have the money to put where your mouth is.)

So we brainstormed for several weeks in Peter's little first floor Standish Street Apartment, pounding beers and working out gags and basically storyboarding the whole thing. Then we'd go our separate ways and write our pieces. If I had to pinpoint what was good about the magazine, when it was any good, I'd say it was that. Either because we were lucid drunks or able in sober moments to decipher drunken inspiration or both, we were able to translate *sessions* that had their own internal logic and rhythm and *joie de vivre*—alright?—into print. Each issue was another dinner party joke, which as everyone knows is all about the delivery.

In the de facto *Squid* office in my third floor garret we'd lay out the magazine … trying by an interplay of pictures and words to recreate something like the flow of conversation.

After scanning the photos with the Nikon and editing them in Photoshop, we'd drop them into the Quark layout and look at a somewhat idealized version of everything on the big two-paged monitor.

(I'd seen what it took to put together a desktop publishing set-up. Back when I lived in Northampton, just before becoming a smuggler, I'd tried to hire myself out as a freelance copy editor, not quite knowing what else to do with a degree in Creative Writing, and was referred to a fellow in Amherst who ran a little DTP outfit. He excitedly explained the need to deliver camera-ready copy, and I interned at his shop for over a year.

(Of course computers were prohibitively expensive. I was so poor, it didn't matter anyway. On top of everything else I had a vague sense back then, call it an intuition, that one had better stay to the main current with all the other little fish driven forward by forces, tides, history.— Later I'd walked into the local Mac retailer and plunked down cash on a new Centris 650; literally plunked four stacks down on the counter, much to the consternation of the sales clerk, who quickly ushered me into a side room to count the money—and continued to spend lavishly on software, scanners, 4-color spreads and large print runs.)

Next we'd print out 11x17 pages on the big QMS laser printer that sat atop a filing cabinet and collate everything, pulses quickening at the lifelike mock-up. (There was still pre-press and running film from a stack of 88MB SyQuest disks and contracting with a printer, but we had a finished draft.)

Pete would get pretty stoked at this point and whip a half-finished beer off the deck, the can skidding forlornly down the street toward Simon's Deli, boarded for the winter, or piss over the railing in an ill-advised joust with the North Atlantic....

The first issue of *Squid* featured an interview Peter did with Arthur Hurray, aka the *Midnight Master*. Arthur was a slight, older gentleman who on Saturday nights would metamorphose for anyone listening to WOMR ("Outermost Radio," indeed) into a psychotic convict.

"There's gonna be shit on the dick or blood on the knife," the Midnight Master growled into the mike, the narrative, by some sort of camp alchemy (or origami), folding in on itself or out of itself before revealing something benign and rather charming, after all. I remember with acid clarity (actually Pete and I were on a psilocybin-inspired brain-storming session) sitting there totally blown away (horrified, in fact), and for some reason The Angels coming into my head and singing *"My boyfriend's back and you're gonna be in trou-ble,"* and seconds later, as if on cue, Arthur cuing the record. ***"Hey la-di-da, my boyfriend's back."***

Sitting in an abandoned beach town after midnight it was what he was *supposed* to play. He knew it and I knew it.

And so Peter and I submitted ourselves to our work—it was what we were supposed to do—and we found no dearth of people willing to help out. It was what they were supposed to do (whether they knew it or not)—so we believed. Thus we bullied them into various stages of drunkenness and dishabille, into writing articles and buying advertising space and generally doing what we asked them.

Whether we were roughing up the cover model in an alley behind the *O.C.* or riding out a hangover in the cabin of a fishing trawler or being carried bodily up the basement stairs of the *Governor Bradford,* we understood that the magazine was a performance, and the harder we performed the better the chance of running the production over to another season....

Our favorite thing was the magazine cover art, which carried over into a semi-nude centerfold (spoof). I suppose that's all very quaint in this age of celebrity cum-face, but it was witty, and provocative, and it woke up the local publishers. Finally we had a lot of people clamoring to get nude for us, which is at least one definition of success.

Several town patriarchs bought ads in the magazine: *Atlantic House* owner and art collector Reggie Cabral, who'd decided to lionize our effort, took his choice of ad space. Here was a man who in his time as local impresario had hosted Sinatra and bailed Jackson Pollock out of the local drunk-tank, taking a personal interest in us. And a severe psychological rupture opened inside me: the truth forcing itself all the time beneath the great lie one lived out in the open, in broad daylight....

Several restaurateurs, a head shop owner and a gallery owner took full pages. *Benetton* took an ad. And *Provincetown Air* was thinking about it. But the formula for roping in big money like American Spirit and Absolut Vodka, who seemed to have back page ads in every glossy, design-inspired publication in the nineties, meant increasing circulation beyond what one could reasonably afford—

then contracting with a distributor who took control of your product, a particular grievance of so many small presses in the era before on-demand printing and e-zines.

It's hard to know what to say. It was honest, earnest work in spite of everything else, and like any love affair it's an incredible effort to talk about once the heart's gone out of it.

There were moments of luck and grace and wit when the work came with ease, and other moments when I had a clear sense I was spending myself on an elaborate and little-comprehended apology.

Finally (this was later) I went on a dress rehearsal of life on the lam. I'd ordered a big press run and rented a van and gone on the road to distribute the magazine throughout the northeast in whatever key locations I could think of: *Newbury Comics* in Boston and *Out of Town News* in Harvard Square; *Record Express* in Northampton and bars and bookstores in Portsmouth and Brattleboro, Hartford and Providence and New Haven. The *MTV* offices in New York.

I remember lying in the back of the van between boxes of magazines, heady smell of printers ink, on a dead Tuesday night on the waterfront in Portland, savoring that old feeling of being alone, anonymous. By this time Perry Mays was surely talking to prosecutors in Chicago, ratting everyone out, whether I knew it or not, and plans were being made for me as I lay there trying to feel safe.

I ran into Courtney Love near *Trash and Vaudeville* on St. Mark's Place and jammed a copy of the magazine into her hand; Courtney, mourning the recent death of her husband, looked down at the magazine uncomprehendingly before politely tucking it under her arm. (Our cartoonist had done a parody of Kurt Cobain's suicide, I realized belatedly.) Then the van got broken into near *KGB Bar*. My friend, a New Yorker, had given me directions to park around the corner from some junkie bazaar, where the van got busted into, fruits of my ill-gotten gain: leather jacket, Dunhill lighter, custom suits, Tumi bag gone, sucked over a kind of event horizon by a collective, yawning hunger. At least they left the magazines. So I fled back to my parents' house in Connecticut shivering, jacketless, the passenger window smashed in, then back to the Cape.

In the end, the publisher of a national art magazine asked me on as editor. No, in the end I got in a shoving match with a transvestite prostitute during an interview in New York, but that's another story.

Our last hurrah, our dirge and swan song, had to be The Great Provincetown Barathon. The idea was for *Squid* staff and closest friends to drink in every bar on Commercial Street—every "important" bar, anyway—a feat that as far as we knew had never been accomplished (or attempted in any conscious or systematic fashion) by O'Neil or Pollock or Mailer or any number of drunken fisherman, and I went at it with half a heart, grown suddenly weary of all my adolescent bullshit. We started out in the East end of town by all the galleries, drinking frozen drinks. By the time we reached the *Surf Club*, not half way through town, I was shit-faced, maudlin.

Peter, my friend and editor, seemed drunk in a way I hadn't seen him before. Like a crab, he generally backed himself into a defensible position from which to transact his business: between a bar rail and pool table in the basement of *The Bradford*; or on the line at the back of *The Blasé*; or cutoff position on a poker table; but he was at large, for the moment, and ricocheting about like a pinball.

In *The Vault,* a supposed S&M club, but as far as anyone could tell a place actually inhabited by shy, forest-dwelling creatures, one girl grabbed a huge dildo and worked it between her tits. We walked into *Front Street* restaurant sans shirts. I cried upstairs at *A-House.* A cook chased us out of *The Old Reliable* with a knife. And by the time we reached *Bubula's* everyone just walked off in different directions.

Masks

I awoke halfway through the front door, flat on my back, feet resting on the threshold, of a cold, Catholic Sunday morning in Massachusetts, December light the color of bricks bruising my face. A solo effort this time. No particular occasion.

After picking myself up and shutting the door, I crawled on all fours to the second floor, then staggered to the third. Morning light blazed through un-curtained sliders like the final judgment, the room buzzed and I fell into bed.

It was after four when I woke, late rays of sun turning colors on the walls.

I took four Advil, drank a couple cups of black coffee, showered, packed, dressed in black jeans, turtleneck sweater and cashmere overcoat and grabbed my Tumi bag.

A cab honked and I took a quick inventory: passport, money, lights out, stuff unplugged. After a brief hesitation at the top of the stairs, I hurried out.

The sun set as we drove across the Province Lands, and the horizon seemed to radiate like a cooling pie crust as we flew across Massachusetts bay to Boston. An hour later I was on a flight to Chicago.

At Water Tower Place on Michigan Ave. I bought a few things for Europe: silver Dunhill Rollagas lighter, dark geometric-patterned Jhane Barnes shirt, My Bloody Valentine CD and Mailer's latest, *Harlot's Ghost,* a weighty tome I ultimately forgot on some connecting flight, nine-tenths of the way through, just as everything was about to be revealed.

You needed a few little trinkets to keep yourself interested. As always, the problem with me was keeping interested. Ever since I was a kid, the further I inquired into a subject the more disillusioned I became at its practical application. Back in college I changed majors three times, starting off as a Poli. Sci.-Econ major and ending up a poet.

I dimly recalled banging away on my Smith Corona late into the night after everyone had abandoned campus for Christmas break freshman year. My term paper for History of the American Labor Movement, an upper level class they let me into, pictured Wobblies beaten and bloodied outside factory gates and argued what I can't remember, though I'm sure it made all the right connection between the forces that broke strikes and the forces that carried out pogroms and lynchings.

… But it's bad manners to point things out like that. Besides, like any serious writer I had no desire to reform humanity, or myself. My only desire was for language—that moment astride your horse.

After college I spent a couple of years in Boston, living like a college student more or less, and generally absorbing as much life as is available to a 23-year old—walking around completely nude, for all intents, fascinated by the rhythm and the shape of things, a shiftless little mouse, the Frederick of that children's book, hoarding colors for some dark winter night.

I had a couple interesting ideas for radio shows at WGBH (before *The Writer's Almanac* was ever conceived), but what they really wanted was for me to get back in the "lockbox" and tally donations....

After moving home for a year to apply to graduate schools and save money, I fit all my things into the back of my little Chevette and one late August day drove up I-95 to the New Hampshire seacoast region, the land flattening out and stretching far away to points north: Kittery, Kennebunkport, Portland, Rockland....

At the Portsmouth rotary I took a winding two-lane highway over tidal inlets and fields fringed with pines to the little town of Durham and parked in a school lot. It was a quiet Sunday afternoon; the main body of UNH students wouldn't be arriving until after Labor Day. I got a $10 haircut and went across the street to Young's Diner to have supper and look through the classifieds for an apartment. After supper I made an appointment from a payphone to see a place and walked around town for an hour or so, then crashed in my car, the evening wet with dew and intimations of frost.

In the rental office the next morning the landlord was chastising three girls who lived in the apartment below the one offered for flooding the bathroom. "All it takes is a little good *hoss* sense," he said, and I knew I'd found the right place. "You're kind of tall," he said to me. "The apartment's in an attic. You might need to stoop."

At the top of a narrow, steep flight of stairs was a long hallway finished in dark bead board, a bright rectangle of sunlight on the wall. At one end was a kitchenette, across from it a bathroom with a half-tub and hose set into a large window gable. At the other end of the hallway was another gable into which I shoved a mattress and stacked all the books I could. Except for weekend trips to Boston or Portsmouth, I spent my 25th winter under the covers reading or hunkered over the little kitchen table writing, the stove turned down low for heat, a bottle of wine and some kind of peasant fare at my right hand.

As part of my Teaching Assistantship I had to take a course in teaching writing, which conflicted with poetry workshop that semester, so I camped outside the Poet's office on the second floor of Hamilton Smith Hall during office hours to see about an independent study.

In the dying light of a late afternoon in September the old building groaned and murmured to itself. Occasionally a loud pop would sound under the stairs. Finally a door banged open and shut on the first floor and there was a shuffling in the hall. A figure in tweed jacket and corduroy trousers hurried into an office and closed the door behind him. After a couple minutes I knocked timorously, a little sheaf of poems in my hand. The door opened and the Poet regarded me with wry amusement.

(I recall him regaling class some time later with his critique of the Creative Writing MFA: *In olden times,* he explained, *you worked on your poems and worked on them, and when you thought you'd got them right, you put them in your pack and made the long trip to the city to see the Master, who if you were lucky, opened the bundle and read the poems, perhaps nodding silently to himself, before sending you back home.*

Simic, our present-day Master, took my poems and began reading, motioning to a chair next to his desk. He turned pages, nodding and occasionally chuckling.

"What can I do for you?" he asked.

During my brief apprenticeship I produced a few poems, a little music. A couple things were published in literary journals. Later a manuscript was a *Juniper* finalist.

My last semester he'd asked my plans. I'd picked up a notion somewhere: "I want to go to West Africa, Abidjan, you know, African rhythms and *je ne sais quois.*"

"Oh, you're looking for *trouble!*" he said….

In Northampton and Provincetown I clung to a college existence. Crime, too, tactfully delayed one's entry into the world, which was half the point, for as soon as you entered the world for real you became yoked to the first job in the first town (with the first girl). Sadly, the simple appeal of that never occurred to me.

As smuggling led me further afield, I thought from time to time about friends who were living normal lives, plugging away at careers, having kids. Their worlds seemed remote. Word would come second-hand of a marriage here, a baby there. You were better off not thinking about them, just as they were better off not thinking about you.

Back in the life, we were at a Club in Brussels. Brad skipped across the dance floor in high heels, making backhanded motions like he was pushing open doors, or arranging invisible gothic tresses, very dramatic. (I will forever remember him singing along with Siouxie Sioux to "Cities in Dust.")

I did an imitation of a man stepping in gum.

Ted, Brian's new boyfriend, possessing all the arrogance of youth, shook dice in his hand, showed you his ass from one side, then the other.

"Hey Brian come here for a minute," I said.

"Yeah?"

"You ready to go?"

We were leaving in the morning. This had been an easy job: Chicago to Brussels and back.

"Yeah."

"We've only got two bags."

"So?"

"You're out."

Brian laughed, blithe spirit.

"No, really, we don't have any bags."

"Ted's gonna be pissed."

"Yeah, well. You tell him."

Brian laughed again.

"You guys aren't in debt or something are you?"

"Not after we get paid."

I was happy for our people. A little money seemed to have inspired everyone to become who they were supposed to become. Brad put his band back together. He and Ted had a cozy domestic arrangement. Claire was restoring a carriage house. I was publishing a magazine. Kyle had a little software start-up. Wasn't realizing one's potential laudable?

Before we got on the plane, Brad twisted one ring then another off his white knuckles and put them in a pouch for me to carry. Then he went through his suitcase throwing out anything that might arouse suspicion or contradict his story. A ticket stub or loose coin could bring down the whole operation.

In the end a smuggler stands for nothing, a mask inside a mask, a means to an end, a series of compromises, deferrals, evasions, substitutions. For a moment, though, everything seemed plausible.

The Golden Age

Claire and I met at *The Blackstone Hotel* in Chicago. The heroin business was flourishing. Couriers came in four days in a row. I met them at the airport and over the next week collected a quarter million.

In fact, this struck me as bad news. I felt exposed. Trouble could come from either end, picking up or delivering, if we didn't get caught ourselves. All it would take was for someone to get snagged somewhere along the line and start talking and we'd be history. It was like we were just waiting for somebody to get caught so we could stop.

I fooled with the idea of making a big move. It would be easy enough to go out on our own: cut a side deal with the Nigerian couriers in Europe who knew the source, and then cut another deal with the Nigerians in Chicago who knew the street; a big score or two, then out. We were pulling in only ten percent of what we could get if we bought in, ten percent of what Alhaji got. For every $65,000 bag of heroin we moved, he'd collect $650,000. That was pretty clear by the sums of money we sometimes smuggled back into Europe: whole garment bags stuffed full. That was the kind of money you could insulate yourself from the world with. The kind we had you invited unwanted attention with, was all. We were hustling essentially, playing a losing game against the clock.

Of course buying in like that would have been going behind Alhaji's back and left us vulnerable to getting ripped off or killed— and it would have brought us into a whole new relation with the law, advancing us to a level we were unwilling to play at. Playing like that would have required us to organize ourselves, body and mind, around a criminal enterprise, and that would have disabused us of the lie, half true, we told ourselves about our innocence— all of it a kind of moral dithering, no doubt, but what of it?

We'd flown to Europe and were waiting out a delay, drinking grog in a half-basement hotel bar—exposed stone foundation, glassed-in fireplace and overstuffed furniture. Snowflakes stuck to the street outside the window.

I turned to Claire. "Let's get out of this," I said.

She looked at me, surprised. I held my gaze.

"Yeah," she said, some deep thought working her jaw.

"Just let's turn everything over to Brad and Ted. Let's just go. We can still keep a cut."

We both sat there thinking. Neither of us said anything more until the next day when we barged in on high-heel Brad. It wasn't even a discussion, really.

Brad just sat there, round-eyed. We didn't even give him a chance to say Yes or No. "You guys have to step up. It's your turn. You get your people, you get Ted and whoever up to speed and then you turn it over to them. We all need to create some distance here." It was actually a reasonable exit strategy, the next best thing to blowing the whole thing up, which would have made the most sense.

"It's yours, Brad. It's yours. When Alhaji calls"—Brad had met him once—"you take the call."

That night, to test Brad and Ted, I called their room. There was no answer. There was no way they could pull this off. Next morning I let them have it. "Don't fuck this up." Then Claire and I left for the airport.

Halfway down the stairs Brad came running after us.

"You've gotta see this."

So we climbed the two flights of stairs and looked into his room; there were clothes strewn everywhere, high heels, total disorder. This new song by Radiohead, "Creep," was on MTV. *Jesus Christ. This is what he wanted to tell us?*

We left and went home. Actually, I went to New York to hang out with an old college buddy, one of two or three people in the world I could unburden myself to. About half a dozen scotch and sodas later I started to feel better, the familiar earthiness of lower Manhattan (and Dewar's) seeping into me.

I called Claire just to touch base. Alhaji wanted us back in Brussels. It had to be a transit job; he needed Claire and me to do it. In fact, he needed people in Jakarta again.

Claire went abroad, and I returned obediently to Chicago. We had responsibilities. Or compulsions, anyway.

It turned out to be the golden age of our little adventure. Claire kept calling me from Jakarta to send more couriers—friends of Brad whom I'd never met. It was funny seeing them come through arrivals. You could spot them a mile away. Waiting in the lobby for couriers to show up was nerve-wracking in its own right, though.

When you went through customs with your couriers, you could see what was going on. When you met them curbside, you had no idea who else might be along.

Of course smuggling is about the smuggling of identity, as much as the smuggling of contraband. The problem, much more pressing than the heroin itself, is suppressing the outward appearance of any knowledge of the heroin....

Most nights I took a taxi up Lake Shore Drive to *Neo*, an industrial goth bar, to work off the angst. It was a small, dark place with a candle-lit bar at the far end of the room, speakers hanging from the ceiling and a couple wooden boxes you could dance on if the spirit moved you. It was a plain kind of place. Nobody seemed to care what you did.

I was dancing—and I have to add I'm not some dancing fool; I really need to get worked up to get out there on the dance floor— I was dancing, minding my own business, when some girl came dancing over. This was entirely out of the ordinary, as it seemed I'd become a species of ghost over the last several months. I was just picking up on it when this guy angled himself between us and boxed me out all broad shoulders, and I was just like, *whatever asshole,* and gave him this little shove, and all of a sudden everything went horizontal. It was dark, and there was heavy breathing in my face, and then this ripping sound, and some brief thrashing about, and suddenly I was yanked back on my feet, not quite sure what had just happened. You couldn't even call it a fight. A tussle, perhaps. A dry-hump? The guy's friends were shaking their heads at him, the bouncers had gone back to the door, business as usual, and I looked down at the sleeves of a man's lightweight sport coat in my hands.

Finally Alhaji told me he couldn't get any more stuff through. I called Claire. She didn't want to come back home. She was going down to Bali to kill time. She had this little Smithie with her,

Temper, whom she was into at the moment, and a couple couriers she'd prematurely sent for, and she was demanding $20,000 or some ungodly sum of money, which I Western Unioned piecemeal to avoid the IRS, who picked up on it anyway.

Claire was yelling at me to go back to Chicago. I couldn't stand it, sneaking off to pay phones to call Bali and Benin in the middle of dinner. There must be a scene like this in every movie, where the guy has to choose between the straight life and *the life* ... and he stashes the stuff in the baby crib, or he misses his own birthday party, or slaps his wife around. I didn't want to be that guy.

Confession

"The way is blocked," Alhaji said, so we took a couple of months off. I told myself this was the end.

The fact is you can't live a double life. As smuggling usurped more and more of my attention, my normal life felt faked. It got so the lying became compulsive. If I had to go to Africa, I told my family I was in Paris. Paris: Chicago. The simple logistic, just the effort to keep time zones straight, was farcical.

And here was L, whom I'd managed to keep as far away from my crimes as possible—whom I'd lied to first out of fear, then out of courtesy to a woman who wanted to believe me—hanging on to me like a drunk by the shirt collar....

For a whole year I'd made one excuse after another: Euro Disney (which was investing in our magazines) had kept us in Paris on a new project. The job was incomplete, blah, blah, blah.

It was New Year's Eve, and we were at our favorite restaurant, Front Street in Provincetown, a cozy brick basement with fishing nets and Tiffany lamps. We'd already had a couple drinks and were waiting for our food. Egged on by liquor, by familiarity, by a sudden conspiratorial impulse, or just plain tired of having this thing between us, I turned to L.

"We've been smuggling heroin for the last year, you know," I said with an absurd grin on my face.

A grave miscalculation.

She just sat there not saying a word as I plunged ahead trying to assemble a jumble of thoughts into a coherent picture, knowing full well my motives were incomprehensible, as the motives of the criminal are ever incomprehensible to the law-abiding and the decent. I pleaded that I wanted to put everything behind me. I was quitting. The more I talked the more hurt she looked.

"That's ... disgusting," she said.

After dinner I drove her home; she'd moved to a little cottage in Wellfleet, sense enough already to stay away.

I called a week later on some pretext, hoping to take the temperature of things. L said to come over. Her little cottage on a sandy lot under tall pines on the side of route 6 was a motel in-season. The screen door banged shut as I walked inside. L was making tea in a down vest. The room was cold and unfamiliar and smelled faintly of mice nests. And looking around at her things: field guides, hip waders, butterfly net, pith helmet, swim fins, it occurred to me that we'd become strangers to one another.

"I need some time to think about things," she said, standing in the middle of the kitchen. "I think you need some time to think about things, too."

"I don't have to think about anything," I said, taking a half step toward her.

"Yes, you do," she said, her voiced choked with disbelief.

"This doesn't have anything to do with my feelings for you."

"I don't know what you feel."

"I love you."

"Well, I don't know what I'm feeling right now."

I waited for her to say something more. She turned and lay the tea bag on the rim of the kitchen sink.

I looked down at the dirty, green carpet.

"I love you," I said.

"That doesn't change things," she said….

It wasn't the first time I drove away from L with tears in my eyes. After that first summer together, when she'd gone back to Northampton and coolly informed me that she was busy with "other things," I'd driven out of town, slamming my fist into the bench seat of the Granada.

I drove away now in a big rush to get home and start drinking.

The New Black

Claire called at some point. She'd taken off on another trip without telling me. She needed me to pick up some money in Chicago and bring it to Brussels. As usual the feeling I might be missing out on the action compelled me to drop everything and go to Europe again.

Claire was still pissed that I'd "left her in Bali." I thought she was losing it. She'd wasted considerable money dragging a lot of people on vacation. Now she had gotten too many *personalities* involved—new girls she wanted to sleep with. The last thing I was interested in was people's *personalities* in the middle of a smuggling trip. And I was irked to learn that she'd sent Brad and Ted, *my* people, down to Jakarta without telling me. Alhaji had said we should wait, so what were we doing in Brussels all over again?

Claire had this new girl with her, Temper, a 23-year-old Smith grad and general pill who worked as a waitress at a local pub. She'd tagged along on the last trip with Claire; the whole $20,000 Bali diversion, I suspected, was to impress her.

Temper could have been a smuggler: by day blonde ponytail, pearls, little cocktail dress from Bergdorf's—except at night something Irish came out: a streak of orange hair, a sharpness of tongue. She called me a pussy once.

Now she hung around the hotel room while Claire and I talked business, the two of them edging onto the bed every few hours to commence their lovemaking.

Cries, moans, little shrieks escaped their throats as they tussled to see who was on top. Claire finally went down on Temper, who whimpered like a Japanese porn actress before she came. Claire sat up with a triumphal look; Temper whipped her hair around, a look of hot shame on her face.

Afterwards, Claire gazed out the hotel window as Temper jogged across the sooty, cobbled square in spandex and splashy cross-trainers, ponytail swinging jauntily. Claire ground out her cigarette.

"Her and that goddamn ponytail," she muttered.

I had no idea women this way could be so adversarial.

All this was just a distraction. The halcyon days of money and hotels and the belief that we'd found an "out" from the drudgery of low wages, meaningless toil and rules were collapsing under their own weight(lessness) and some vaguely felt second act in which we might be called upon, if only by our own brains, to speak for ourselves, not legally or ethically, but existentially—as we all must—was being wheeled into place. You could smuggle drugs or whatever, but refuse the hand of fate....

We were still in Brussels, waiting on Alhaji's call. Everyone was drinking in a discotheque across the square. Claire and Temper and

Zane and some new boy who kept holding out the sleeve of a sweater for me to touch were sitting on barstools at a high table filled with drinks.

I couldn't seem to get properly drunk, couldn't find that sweet spot and was on my fifth drink now; and the faces around me were grinning ... as if to assert their reality ... against my own. *Against my own!* I lurched forward, rocking the table. A goblet of wine stood on edge; everyone's attention fastened on the glass like a roulette ball or a spinning bottle. Then the table rocked back the other way and the glass stood on its other edge. The table rocked a third time and the glass flipped over and the wine shot straight onto this boy's sweater, blood staining a field of heathers. "Oh!" he cried, like he'd been struck. "Oh!" the others cried. I sat there nodding, a grin slowly taking shape on my face.

Later that afternoon I walked, drunk, through the *Musee d'Arte Moderne* in Brussels, down a winding white hallway to some inner recess. In a corner, behind glass, a little ventriloquist's dummy in baggy pants and jacket sat before a brass bell. For minutes on end he just sat there with his feet sticking out in front of him, like he'd been knocked down in the street. Then something seemed to stir inside him and the doll's torso jerked forward an inch and its metal head—*bang!* struck the bell producing an unexpectedly bright peal like the bell of a steamship. A little placard read, "**Attempt to Raise Hell.**" *Dennis Oppenheim. American.*

A small group waited in anticipation for it to happen again. Just as a couple turned to walk away, *bang!* the bell clanged again. I stayed for another half hour listening to the intermittent clanging; the little brute kept at it, as if he had a mind of his own—as if, in spite of whatever wind-up mechanism controlled him, he was determined to carry out this errand he alone knew the meaning of.

When I arrived back at the hotel, Claire was arguing with some guy in the hallway whom she'd picked up at the disco then had second thoughts about. He stood there, aggrieved, long hair and ripped jeans, trying to push his way back into the room. I was in the process of telling him to fuck off when he spit right in my face. I stood there blinking as he ran down the three flights of stairs to the street. Then I ran after him and caught him fumbling with his keys in front of the hotel.

He turned to face me.

"Get the fuck out of here," I screamed.

He looked back at me stupidly, long hair hanging in his face.

"You better get the fuck out of here," I said in a tremulous voice. For a second it looked like he was going to spit again, and in an access of rage I grabbed him and threw him bodily down onto the sidewalk. He grabbed his hip in pain and scampered into his car, revved the engine insanely, and peeled out on the cobblestones.

Back in the hotel room, Temper was sitting on Claire, pinning her wrists. From behind you could see their pubic mounds touching. I poured myself a Grand Marnier and sat on the couch. Temper pretended to clear her throat and let hang a loogie over Claire's face.

Heroin was coming; I didn't know when. For some reason Claire was being cagey. She didn't know, either. So I went on auto-pilot, certain that this thing didn't work without the two of us pulling together—as much as she wanted to believe or I wanted to believe or anyone else wanted to believe otherwise.

Claire and I worked well together, not that we necessarily complimented one another. Our relationship was based more on a mutual recklessness. We drove one other, achieving a kind of collective force. (When I told her I wanted to get out on the last trip, she went along out of habit, until Alhaji reeled us back in to do the transit job and Claire came to her senses and started jamming through couriers again, redoubling her efforts in Indonesia and refusing to come home. I'd faltered. I'd said No.)

Claire had no intention of quitting. Whether she was unswayed by reason, like me, or had in fact envisioned some end zone in which she might simply drop the ball and walk away after running up the score, I don't know. Most likely she was just caught up in a moment that was impossible to sustain, or let go of.

We never did quite know what to do with the money. How to hide it. So we each invested in a project that was dear to us. I dumped money into *Squid* magazine. Claire restored a carriage house on some friends' property outside Brattleboro, Vermont—and I suppose I was jealous in a way: while Claire was building equity, I was speculating.

On top of that, Claire was always calling in a panic: *The contractor needed more money or he was going to walk off the job. The roof was half-finished and it was going to rain.* She needed cherry cabinets or marble counter tops or dry river stones for the fireplace—*they had to be dry for twenty years.* So I "lent" her the money without complaint. Invariably, in a matter of weeks or months we'd be abroad again, lining up another payday.

You always needed more money. That was the way the world worked, the criminal world as well as the straight world. It was this belated realization that we were involved not in some kind of counter-culture, but another business that organized human endeavor in the service of capital, that rankled.

The trip turned into a long waiting game. This was the worst part of the job. You could run out of money after a week or two waiting for some bags that might never show, all the while trying to keep nervous, suspicious people happy. In the midst of this, Claire and I started to bicker. She mentioned the old term "god's work."

"What the fuck are you talking about? We're smuggling *heroin!*" I shouted at her.

"That's not what this is about!" she yelled right back, without missing a beat.

"Oh, right, this is humanitarian work we're doing, I forgot."

"You shut up," she said through clenched teeth.

After that we retreated to separate corners. Claire and Temper whispered conspiratorially. I buried my head in a book.

Finally Alhaji called and said that the only way he could get us bags was in transit. So, on the appointed day, Temper, Claire and I along with a couple other couriers went to the airport in Brussels. We were at a far end of the transit lounge standing against a wall.

A familiar-looking African in a Fila baseball cap came over with another guy, put the bags down and lit a cigarette.

"Hey, how are you guys doing?" he said, smiling.

"Good, good, man," I said, trying to strike the casual note. "How was the trip?"

"No problem. Alhaji says to call from the other side."

The people we met in transit were usually pretty competent; Africans who took the bags as far as was safe, usually Western Europe, Brussels in particular. These were Alhaji's people. They inspired calm, unlike when the bags got farmed out in Jakarta to sweating persons who looked like they'd been on a plane for about 23 hours.

As the two Africans walked away, we looked down at the suitcases. Two bags. Three couriers.

Temper stepped forward. Claire shook her head, *No*, gesturing for the other two to grab the bags—not so much out of a desire to protect Temper, it seemed to me, as to keep her in her place, and Temper responded with all the choler of the little sister who's been told she can't hang out with the big kids.

She hissed. She stamped her foot.

Claire assumed an attitude of wounded dignity.

They argued back and forth in plaintive tones, fists clenched at their sides.

"Tell her to shut up," I finally said to Claire, the two of them looking up, blushing. And I decided right then and there that I'd had it with the whole fiasco.

Safely stowed aboard the plane, we made our way back to Chicago without further incident, came through customs, took a cab into town, checked into a hotel and made the exchange.

Everyone was dancing at Octagon: Ted shaking dice and showing his ass, Brad in high heels arranging invisible gothic tresses, and Temper stomping in puddles. I couldn't seem to make my feet move. Claire wasn't talking.

I went out on the street and looked at the single-story brick buildings. Low clouds scudded off the lake, and the light shifted, turning everything sepia.

If you'd asked just then what I thought I was doing standing out on the street drunk like that in the middle of the afternoon, I would've said without irony or self-deception that it wasn't me.

—*You got the wrong guy, pal.*

The Muffin Man

Back home I fretted over *Squid* magazine. We were short on funds, but we weren't prepared to give up just yet. There was still something I wanted to say, something I'd once felt that eluded me at the moment, but if we gave up now, what would the point have been? All that risk, for what? You're in a burning building, what do you do: run out the front door empty-handed or save your leather coat, your books, your hard drive—all those things that give your life shape and coherence? So one night I called Alhaji and told him I was going out on my own, not with Claire any longer. "I had two people," meaning I wanted two bags of heroin.

Alhaji wanted me to sort out things with Claire, first. Of course Claire used this as a pretext to extract more money from me, asking for $10,000 as "tribute" to her sister, Hester, who after providing us with an entrée into the whole business of heroin smuggling had receded into the background, too flakey to play it straight for long, and another five for her own machinations. Claire was going to San Francisco with Temper to set up a "recruiting house." *Brilliant. Fine, whatever.* Once again, the cost of doing business. The cost of cutting ties.

When Alhaji called back with the go-ahead I took a Ptown guy who'd hung around long enough and gotten hungry enough and whose affinity for crime stories had gotten him hankering after the real thing, and Ted, to Zurich. I fretted about bringing him along. I'd tried to keep smuggling separate from my "real" life, but those lines were beginning to blur. In truth I'd pretty much ceased functioning with anything like a conscience and merely came blowing through people's lives like a rain squall.

Wandering through the airport in Zurich in a black concert tee and canvas high tops, Peter wound up getting a stamp on his passport, which was a problem. It was supposed to be a quick turnaround, a mop-up job, two bags in transit and home. I called Alhaji. He said only one bag was coming. Ted, ever the consummate professional, came into the room and enquired "Hair up or down," went to the airport, picked up the bag and flew home to Chicago.

Peter and I waited. Then we waited some more; killed time drinking and watching TV.

On the day of departure we arrived at the airport in Zurich with plenty of time to spare and went to get the bag. This involved finding an African, sidling alongside and exchanging bags.

The airport wasn't too crowded, mid-morning weekday, and I meandered around the area in which we'd done most of our exchanges. Bright sunlight shone through floor-to-ceiling windows at the end of the terminal. Nothing so far.

There's an ebb and flow in an airport. Flights arrive and the passengers filter into the terminal, find their bags and leave. Then another flight arrives a little while later.

The arrivals board said that a flight from Nigeria had landed about an hour earlier, so I sauntered to the far end of the terminal and back but didn't see any Nigerians at all. I killed a little time flipping through magazines in a newsstand. Too nervous to stand still for long, I resumed my walk.

Finally someone with a bag that looked about right set his bag down next to a kiosk. I came up next to him and put my bag down. Nothing. I stared hard at him. No recognition. I left the bag and took a couple steps away. Still nothing. This wasn't our guy.

It was getting late. Boarding would begin in another hour. The bag had to be here somewhere.

I took another lap around the terminal, starting to panic. Two machine-gun toting police strutted along an overhead catwalk. *What must this all look like to anyone watching?* I wondered.

Finally I got a phone card and went to a pay phone and called Alhaji.

"The bag's not here," I said.

"That is not possible."

"What do you mean? It's not here. I can't find it."

"The other side called to say you received the bag."

"What?"

"They say you picked up the bag."

"Who said?"

"The boy told his boss."

"You … Alhaji, you know me. I can't find the bag. I didn't pick any bag up."

"Don't leave. Look around again."

I looked around again and again. Nothing. My phone card was dead and I was out of money, so I called on a credit card.

"They can't find the boy," he said. "He must be on a plane. You should have called sooner."

"I thought … I don't…."

"Go back to your hotel and stay there."

This was bad.

We left the airport and headed back into Zurich. Shortly after, Alhaji called and told us to change hotels, so we packed up and skulked down a back staircase and walked along the canal for a couple blocks and then went back up a side street and checked into a new hotel.

I called back later that day. Alhaji said I should remain in Zurich until things got sorted out.

"Nicky," he said with little or no preamble, "if I am in the fire, then you are in the pepper."

"What do you mean?"

"I mean you're in this," he said.

As the week wore on Peter and I got drunker and drunker, our daily sense of reality beginning to skitter off center like a dusty needle on a record. By noon we'd be drunk in the hostess bars. Pete was crying over some Svetlana…. At one point this fellow started following us. I did a quick in and out of a bar, and passed him coming back out. Probably just some queer, but at the time you imagined they were onto you.

Then Peter started complaining about breakfasts. "You know," he said. "if I could just get a normal breakfast or something. A muffin or something."

"A muffin?" I said.

"Yeah," he said.

And I sang in a whiny sing-song: "Do you know the muffin man, the muffin man, the muffin man?"

—"Yeah," I said, in my best Andrew Dice Clay-voice, "I *fucked* him."

Fetish Oath

Standing on a street corner late at night, moonlight and frost on the cobblestones, thinking *Just give me a sign, God,* I took one step and went skidding on a pile of dog crap of a size and foulness not to be believed, smearing shit in the side zipper of my stylish high-heeled Amsterdam clogs. Next morning I called Alhaji. "Two people," I said, disdainful of the obvious symbolism—stepping in shit and all....

Peter was gone, I was alone in Zurich. Alhaji had called to say he wanted to put another run together. It all felt wrong.

That night I made my way to an after-hours bar on a dead-end street with a fat man, a hooker and a bouncer at the end of the bar moving around cases of beer. I leaned back in my chair making cracks. The place looked like something out of *The Deer Hunter,* a steelworker bar. Everything went into slow motion. I was blacking out.

Suddenly, without warning the bouncer was jabbing me and the fat guy in the chest, pointing outside. The fat guy turned sheepishly to go, which only seemed to incite the bouncer, who slapped him upside the head, and finding the result satisfactory, slapped him twice more in quick succession like a cat, then kneed the fat man in the coccyx bone, straightening him back up, and violently shoved him through the door, a miracle of efficiency; then before I could get out the door, too—because it seemed to me it was time to go now—he locked it shut and brushed quickly past, locked the inner door and spun around, his face a mask of grief and rage, as if someone had made a cutting observation about his personal appearance, or laughed at him, which maybe they had.

I was half expecting some kind of explanation when he slammed me in the gut with a terrific punch. The wind went out of me in a rush and I felt a warm release. I couldn't stop it, nor did I want to. *Just stay on your feet,* I thought, and half bent over raised my hands in a gesture of surrender.

There was a cab waiting by the door. I got in and rolled the window down, sat back in my seat and lit a cigarette with steady hands. I'd had it coming for some time now, with my shitty attitude and my transgressions, and a total feeling of well-being enveloped me. A feeling of victory.

In a couple of days Brad and Ted, whom I'd come to call "The Goddamn Professionals," were back in Zurich. We were heading to *Cote d'Ivoire*.

Stepping out of the Abidjan Novotel onto Avenue de Gaulle you stepped from Europe to Africa in a single bound. Glass and concrete and tree roots intermingled freely.

Banks, French multi-nationals and the government occupied blocks of high-rises. Single story concrete buildings with steel shutters crowded between. Across the street from the hotel a restaurant with bright orange walls and waiters in white shirts and aprons animated the street.

This was the Goddamn Professionals first time in Africa and they were looking a little pasty, so I dragged them over to a guy cooking plantains under a tree in the middle of the street and plopped down on a log. In no time we were eating with a group of old men and neighborhood kids, promising little Oliver, an enterprising eight-year-old, that we'd buy his little carvings of *la famille de fruits* before we left. As we ate the piping hot plantains, Oliver chatted happily away in English and French, displaying his little carvings of apples and bananas, which he kept wrapped in an oil cloth.

Then Alhaji summoned me to Benin. There was going to be an oath of some sort over the missing heroin.

At the Beninese consulate in Cocody, a diplomatic neighborhood on a hill across the lagoon, a minor row was going on. A sheepish looking man and woman of lower middle-class appearance came rushing out of an immaculate little house pursued by a pissed-off looking functionary who harangued them all the way across the manicured lawn, telling them not to come back without the proper fee, of course.

He smiled as if he'd been expecting me, led me inside and processed my visa in ten minutes flat, and I caught a flight later that day.

In Benin, Alhaji was standoffish. I tried a joke to get a rise out of him. He knew I didn't steal a bag. I wanted him to tell me everything would be okay.

"Get some sleep Nicky. Tomorrow we will go into the bush and take an oath with the marabout. There is still a problem with the bag."

That night I lay in bed going over everything in my head. Obviously the boy's story held and they were inquiring into me. Either he was lying and had stolen the bag of heroin, or someone else had. I just couldn't imagine what third party might have swooped in like that. Who would be privy to that information. Who I had told. Some vague suspicion kept whispering that it was all too simple, it was right in front of me. But I just couldn't see it.

The next morning I went to get in the car with Alhaji. "You go with the driver," he said, motioning behind him to a compact Daewoo from his car dealership. The sleeve of a beautiful white *agbada* fluttered. Then Alhaji turned and climbed behind the wheel of a big BMW.

We drove out the gates of the compound in the fashionable Cotonou suburb, along the coast to Porto Novo and north into the interior. After a while we pulled over to the side of the road and waited; a car came down a gated drive and fell in behind Alhaji. A little later another car. Farther still, as we were going through a small town, some skinny dude jumped off the back of a motorcycle and climbed in the lead car with Alhaji. These, it seemed to me, were the conglomerate of families involved in moving heroin from Asia to the U.S., each group with an interest in the shipments of heroin, and each swallowing their portion of the loss—an initial investment of some tens of thousands, I guessed, and lost profit in the hundreds of thousands; but more important, lost trust.

At one point Alhaji slowed and waved us alongside.

"How are you doing, Nicky?"

I was wondering, in fact, if I should have contacted the American embassy. Of course stealth had been the rule all along: moving in and out of countries, careful to use a clean passport without entry or exit stamps, calling from phone booths and all the onerous business of crime.

I made a face of mock horror; Alhaji laughed and drove on. All I could do now was sit back in my seat and watch the huge landscape go by—and think about the oath, which bore no thinking about at all if one were to approach it with a clear head, not that that mattered either. Voodoo has voodoo logic, a deterministic kind of logic; it wasn't the dice roll that determined your fate, but your fate that determined the dice.

Anyway, in my brief experience with *vodun* I'd encountered some things that defied easy explanations. One time Alhaji took me and Claire to this Church to see a big fat lady witch doctor who gave us candles for safe travel. We were in Benin for only three days because it was Thanksgiving—I remember Alhaji's cook had made the toughest turkey ever; I twisted the drumstick three full turns before it broke free of the carcass, Claire and Alhaji laughing and cheering me on—and flew straight back from Africa, rather than through Europe, so they stopped us in Customs in New York, strip-searched me, x-rayed my shoes, the whole nine yards, only they couldn't find the stub of a candle the witch doctor had given me in the inside breast pocket of my jacket.

Another time Alhaji invited us to Benin to discuss business. Things hadn't been going so well. Claire and I were at odds. The novelty of being a drug smuggler had worn off. Alhaji had asked us to Benin to discuss business, though what "business" consisted of was never quite clear. Often as not he just wanted to show off his *oyibos*, his Whities.

There were two marabouts at the house doing the usual witch-doctoring thing. That evening I lay in bed listening to them as they chanted from different parts of the house, first one then the other; they went on without regard for what the other was doing, their rhythms crossing back and forth, rubbing together for an instant before sorting themselves back out. And I fell asleep and went into a dream. In the dream I was struggling with something. For long moments I tried to wake, and I sat up with a scream caught in my throat. The next day the problem was gone, whatever it was.

We were three hours or more into the bush now—rolling, dry backcountry of West Africa, void of any kind of life as far as the eye could see. Only occasionally smoke from a cook fire lazily threaded the branches of a distant tree. Someone was burning the trunk of a fallen palm for wine, driving out the sap. When it was fermented he'd scoop the cloudy, sweet drink out of a zinc pail with a tumbler, waving away flies—boil it through a copper coil to make gin afterwards.

At last we began to slow down. A whirlwind whisked a little branch from the side of the road and held it mid-air. I was staring at this strange thing. Was it a simple whirlwind? Or was I just spooked?

A few miles down the road we drove past a black crucifix. *This must be the place.*

And turning off the highway we went into a little town. There was a neat little square, an ancient acacia tree, some wooden buildings without windows, like storage rooms or granaries. A fetish wandering blind in a great papier-mache head.

We followed the road past the little town and turned down another pitted road, dry branches scraping at the side of the car. (I am trying to conceptualize all this as on a map, but it is as obscure as a snail's track.)

Finally the road ended. Six Africans stepped out of cars, replacing *kufis* and throwing sleeves of kaftans over their shoulders so the hems didn't drag on the ground. They conferred briefly. Then one fellow pointed to a thicket.

A force of will, perhaps not my own, carried me on shaky legs down into a gulley of thorn bushes to a low, red mud hut, which they made me wait outside of. Then I was ushered inside and directed to sit. It took a moment for my eyes to adjust. The marabout—the *babalawo,* the ju-ju man—was squatting on the floor, staring into a little pink plastic mirror with the dried husk of a cocoon bound to the front of it, drinking African gin from a scarred glass.

I squatted on the floor and he turned and stared into my face, a fleeting curiosity on his part. He frowned. Then it was as if a curtain had dropped and he had slipped away.

The Nigerians sat on a low bench, murmuring together. Everyone treated the marabout with great respect. A heavy African in designer sunglasses nodded his head as the marabout tossed cowry shells in a rusty pie tin. Another fellow with gold rings looked on narrowly.

None of them, neither Alhaji nor the others, looked at me. It was like they weren't there; or I wasn't there, watching through a one-way mirror.

The marabout tossed the shells again, tossed them a third time, regarding the pattern they made; and it occurred to me he only wanted to know if I was *lucky,* not merely truthful, which is a human notion and therefore suspect, but lucky—*ire,* itself, a proper African virtue underlying one's relation to the forces of nature, the Orishas, the powers, which Africans revere above all else, and telling not so much if I stole the bag (or Alhaji stole the bag or Claire stole the bag or some guy from the other side stole the bag) but who would be held to account, which was the point; and what *were* the Orishas whispering through those shells? I wondered.

The marabout began to speak.

After a moment the skinny dude who'd jumped off the motor-cycle interjected.

The marabout said something.

Alhaji said something.

The marabout said something else.

"The bag!" the guy with designer glasses shouted in English.

The marabout repeated what he said.

It was like an explosion of voices, everyone shouting "The bag! The *bag!*"

The Marabout spoke a different dialect of Yoruba. There was shouting in French, English.

Exasperated, the marabout waved them off.

Alhaji said something to the fellow with the rings now, who said something back. Then the fellow with the glasses chimed in energetically, and the three talked for several minutes.

I listened to the back-and-forth, hung on every word, every inflection, trying to suss out the argument. A crowd of little kids had gathered at windows carved into the earthen hut, but if they understood anything that was going on, their blank faces revealed nothing.

The skinny dude was voicing his opinion in a surprisingly deep voice, all m's, b's and p's and round o's and short a's. I was sweating profusely in a dark red, long-sleeved shirt. Still no one would look at me.

I searched the ground for something to use as a cudgel, or stab with, but quickly abandoned the idea as foolish, here—three hours in the middle of the bush, friendless and a sea.

I'm sorry L, I didn't mean it to come to this....

Alhaji was arguing forcefully now. The others listened. Some sort of tension had released.

Then Alhaji turned to me. "I think everything is going to be okay, Nicky. I will fight for my side. I will win. Now you will take an oath."

Everyone stood and walked out of the hut into white light. In a little swept clearing someone shook out a white sheet, which we held over our heads as we sat on the ground.

The marabout led everyone in a call and response. My lips moved dully along. Then Alhaji recited an oath, line by line, for me to repeat.

"I give my loyalty to Alhaji ... I understand that as long as I remain loyal, nothing can happen to me ... I will never say anything against Alhaji or any of his people, and no one can harm me."

After the recitation, the marabout stuck a thorn into a muddy concoction and before I understood what was happening pressed it into my wrist.

Great, I thought. *I'm made.*

Or dead.

A Lie too Far

I got in the car with Alhaji, leaned back in my seat and lit a cigarette.

Alhaji glanced over at me.

Dried sweat rimed the front of my shirt and face.

What had I'd just seen? Had I been admitted on some level? Was I changed? Was I wiser?— Was this where Alhaji reached into the glove compartment and pulled out CIA credentials or a gun or removed a glass eye? I wondered, feeling that a revelation of some sort were in order.

"I want you to be sure your people are ready," he said, watching the road in front of him.

"Sure," I said.— My people were never ready. Fistfights, brass bands, self-urination we had aplenty; readiness not so much.

"You can tell them they are carrying documents," he said.

I looked at him driving low in the seat. Of all the lies I'd told, this was too much.— I might lie about where I was or what I'd been doing because it wasn't anybody else's business really. (A source of my discontent it seemed to me was the way the world crowded in amongst you, demanding answers: *Whose birthday gift? Whose cigarette?*) Lying to couriers, however, robbed them of free-choice. (If this over-concern made me an amateur, it was also my final defense.)

I started to object and stopped. It was a breach of etiquette, no doubt, to introduce personal feelings where they didn't belong. Whatever your ethical point of view, you kept it to yourself. It was irrelevant; a luxury none of us could afford.

If I really wanted to force the point, my lack of professionalism was the real failing, compared to Alhaji, who managed always to keep his hat on straight.

And I thought about his role in this, a Nigerian and Yoruba who seemed to have leaped out of time, trailing apocrypha: hustling cars and dealing drugs at Jinson Motors back in the day, busting out of jail in Lagos and making his way to Benin. Did he have a wife? *Wives?* Children?

I watched the scenery rewind, the roughness of the interior giving way to level tracts. Did he have an old father somewhere— a cab driver or civil servant who had imparted to his son the habit of keeping abreast of things? Or was it a mother, perhaps, the elder wife of a successful merchant who kept the others under her thumb with Egyptian guile whilst carving out a small place for her son, who had shaped him? Or a tragic elder brother-figure, a precursor to Alhaji, gunned down in the street?

Like the rest of post-colonial Africa, he seemed self-invented. He showed you only as much as he wanted to, but in that he had a theatrical flair, as the oath exemplified.

Sometimes he seemed to have reasons. Sometimes I saw no reason at all, other than a desire to put one over on us.

The previous evening when I'd arrived at the house there was a man sitting in a chair next to a reading lamp in the middle of the living room.

"I want you to remember his face," Alhaji said cryptically.

The man looked straight ahead as I studied his profile. Then he glanced at me furtively as I turned toward Alhaji.

"What are you looking at!" Alhaji savaged him.

"I am sorry, sir!" the man quickly replied looking at the ground before being turned out of the house.

A stifled belch rose up in Alhaji's esophagus and be exhaled forcefully through the nose.

It was absurdist theater; a new, unrelated episode thrust into the play each time things made sense....

The car sped back through the bush. An interminable midday sun beat down on the dusty road, scattering parabolas of light, and I found myself nodding off in my seat. I bit down hard on my lip and stared through the windshield. It was no use fighting it, and I gave myself over to sleep like a prey in the paw of a big cat.

I woke some time later as we approached Porto Novo on the coast. Light shone through the trees. Alhaji pulled onto the side of the road where a man was selling roasted ground nuts.

"Eat something, Nicky," he said as he came back to the car holding two little paper cones.

And we sat there munching peanuts, watching people walking back from work along a little worn path, possessed of a sense ... hindsight perhaps ... of an ending: a long, floating moment before time moves forward again, toward some other purpose.

"Is everything okay?" I said

"I think everything will be okay, Nicky."

"I hope so," I said.

"There is still a problem with the bag."

Blitzed

The next morning, before Binga drove me to the airport, I joined Alhaji at breakfast, where he was fussing over a bowl of corn flakes.

"Do you believe in God?" Alhaji asked out of the blue.

"Sure," I said.— In my experience, the person asking that question is looking for affirmation.

"You cannot do this work if you don't believe in God," he said.

"Okay," I said.

"You cannot," he repeated axiomatically.

On the flight back to Ivory Coast I puzzled briefly over what he meant by "God." I supposed he'd meant *constancy*, or obedience, perhaps, to an idea or organizing principle, ours of course being the heroin conspiracy that bound us together—though it seemed to me he little appreciated how much we'd all come to hate one another.

*

Who knows what they did to me in the bush. Wandering the marketplace in Abidjan in a daze, I attracted a crowd of waifs who harassed me all the way back to the hotel. In the air-conditioned safety of the Novotel lobby, I peered back through the fogged glass. A dozen or more children beckoned on the sidewalk. I turned to the manager in appeal.

The manager, an African, gestured piteously to the crowd. (One so rarely understood the stakes here.)

Outside, I emptied my pockets and then went upstairs to lie down....

Abidjan is the third largest French-speaking city in the world and like any big African city that takes in its share of refugees from drought, famine, civil war, etc., petty sometimes violent crime is inevitable.

When you walked out of your hotel at night the buildings were shuttered. Streetlights shed feeble circles of light at long intervals. And in the distance the street went dark. You stood there, equivocal, impelled by the mystery of Africa: the possibility that at every turn the miraculous might appear—some primitive come striding through the crowd naked, cock swinging like a hammer, holding a baby baboon or a carving of incomparable strangeness and beauty; and you were simultaneously driven back by the fear that you were not strong enough for what lay ahead, that it would break your heart.

I hired a driver and stuck to him. Dumbwie, was an older fellow who wanted to show me Africa. He'd invited me to his village to his Uncle's funeral, but I had to stay by the phone. I had business—one of my biggest regrets about my travels, but we drove around the city and went to restaurants where we ate big bowls of *Kedjenou*, chicken and vegetables and tomato and couscous in clay pots. We drove out to a nightclub in Treichville, dark hills against the evening sky, deep fragrances all around as we raced down an unlit highway in his cab.

This was against the rules. You absolutely didn't want anyone catching on to what you were doing—and it was hard when you were on a trip; it was like people got a whiff of your adrenaline. The gears didn't mesh.

The next morning I went for a walk through the Plateau district of Abidjan, where we were staying. Across Avenue de Gaulle a field of weeds and broken concrete crumbled into a steep depression. A staircase led down to a patchwork of sheets and blankets shading market-goers from the blazing sun. In the dim stalls—one can't help but think of Conrad—you began to recognize in so-called masks not the guise, but the true human gaze: greed, horror, grace, dignity wooed from wood.

A couple merchants dunned me with their wares. You sensed the adjacent vendors listening, probing for weakness. I merely said "No," and continued to examine carvings, bolts of fabric, refusing to be routed because if you let them do that you wound up with a little pack of gamin harassing you all the way back to your hotel.

Then Alhaji called; *time to move.* The plan was the Goddamn Professionals, Brad and Ted, would fly from Ghana to Switzerland. At a stopover in Lagos, two Nigerians would board with the bags. Brad and Ted would take the bags in the air, then when they landed pass them to a second group in the transit lounge in Zurich. The second group would deliver the bags to Chicago. That was the plan, except Brad and Ted were pretty freaked out when they heard. The idea of flying into Ghana by themselves and staying for a couple days sorely tested their imaginations, and the in-air switch was a new wrinkle, on top of which Alhaji had given me half a hundred-dollar-bill that Brad needed to match up with the Nigerians' half. It was just one thing too many. Brad said *No*, they didn't want to go.

"No way, no way," Ted said angrily, standing in the middle of the hotel room crossing his arms.

Brad was more conciliatory. "We can't. I have to go home," he said.

In fact he looked ill. His hands trembled as he lit a cigarette.

"I don't want to go," he said, looking down. Then he was silent, and I knew he was waiting for me to finish the argument.

"It's a little late for that, Brad."

"I don't care," he said, tears in his eyes.

"Come on, Brad. We'll be done with this in a minute and we'll be back home and we'll all go out dancing at *Neo*."

Brad looked back at me. And his silence was another kind of argument.

My eyes replied in kind: *You two are going to pack your bags and you're going to fly to Ghana; you're going to do this, you goddamn professionals.*

In the bright light of the hotel window, a host of emotions played over his face: disbelief, sorrow, anger. *I'll do this,* his look finally said. *But it's all over between us.* (The inevitable outcome amongst conspirators.)

On the day I left, little Oliver, whom we'd befriended on the first day in Abidjan, met me at the airport, regaling me in French and English: "*Ca va,* brother?" he said, gaily, taking his carving of *la famille de fruits* from the little oil cloth he kept them in.

"*Ki lon sele?*" I said, mistaking the Yoruba phrase.

After choosing some carvings, I gave him all my *francs* and said goodbye, vaguely depressed at how the business of smuggling heroin seemed always to preclude full and free disclosure of human feeling—depressed that it was all a just a front.

Of course now that I'd given away all my money, customs tried to exact a "fee" from me. Having watched Alhaji's summary dealings with all the officious little persons you encounter in Africa, I wagged my finger *No* in the cop's face. So he gave me a twenty

(American) to get him a bottle of Johnny Walker from the duty free shop. Traveling in Africa you learned how the world worked, stripped of its conceits. In the end it was all *quid pro quo*, just the terms were different.

After a little wait the plane took off for Europe. Everything was in motion. Brad and Ted were now on their flight from Ghana to Switzerland. The new recruits were waiting for us in the transit area.

I tried to remember what it felt like to lead a normal life, not scared to death half the time—to be an ordinary traveler going home for the holidays....

The plane landed in Zurich. Nobody was there. Nothing. Nobody. No couriers, no bags. No Brad or Ted. No Africans. The whole scene had a horrible sense of deja vu. Time to call Alhaji. *"Alhaji n'est pas la,"* the voice said.

Not sure what else to do, I headed back into town to the Hotel Rathaus. Out of curiosity I checked a few aliases. Sure enough, everyone was together, napping, nursing frayed psyches in eiderdown. The Nigerians never showed with the bags, so everyone smartly exited the airport in Zurich and holed up here.

I lay on the carpet listening to the radiator's faint ticking. After Africa, Europe seemed absurdly orderly—the only semblance of dirt, dust motes swirling in the window.

A day or so later Alhaji finally answered the phone and said to put everyone back in place for another try, no explanation what happened on the other end. Maybe I should have been more inquiring.

The Goddamn Professionals, Brad and Ted, headed back to Ghana, driven by fear and adrenaline now. Walking to their cab they seemed to huddle together like a couple of retirees in aloha shirts boarding the wrong bus, and my heart ached for a minute.

The new guys, whose job it was to take the bags back to Chicago, stayed in Zurich. I'd met Perry before. The fucking guy groped me in the basement of a punk club in Chicago. I'd told Brad no way would he ever work for us. But all of a sudden we needed bodies, so here he was, a proverbial unlucky penny, red-faced and wheezing. He'd made an unsuccessful attempt to coiffure his thinning hair, and he smelled of day-old cologne.

Carl, in contrast, was tall and handsome and composed, like a German film actor.

Generally the rule was we stayed to ourselves, but these guys were thirty and self-responsible, I figured. Perry had a college friend who lived in a Zurich suburb who'd invited us to dinner, and a little *normalcy* seemed like a good thing—except it wasn't, really.

Tramping into the little condominium Perry's college pal owned, I felt like a lout. Here in the company of the European middle-class: young husband, wife and child, a picture of familial good-will, came I. What was I? Whatever it was, it wasn't nice, and I barely made any effort to conceal it: shook hands, ate dinner, gave the most cursory answers to what was asked and after dinner excused myself and walked up a hill outside the little development and sat under some trees, sullenly smoking beneath a glowering, gray sky.

Back in Zurich, Perry and Carl and I drank every night. Perry talked on and on, and I soon came to recognize something reckless in him.— Of course it was that way with everyone: they weren't on board a minute and already they were talking shit. Kyle, Temper, now Perry. I guess being a drug dealer bred a mutual contempt. Still, I had the feeling that I needed to assert myself.

"If anyone ever got arrested," Perry said, slurring his words.

"Yeah?"

"I get it."

"Get what?"

"I get it."

"What do you get?"

"What happens."

"What do you think happens?"

"Aw, you know."

"No, I don't know, tell me."

"Hey, listen. I'm a big boy."

I waited for him to finish his thought.

"I'm just saying."

"What?"

"I'm just saying."

"What?"

"I'm just saying that we're all friends, I get that."

Yeah, we were all friends, possessing all the murderous impulses of friends....

One evening we were sitting by the window of our hotel room when a real brass band pushed its way down the cobbled street—the strains of "Inagodadavida" played by tubas and trombones and a fellow dressed as a bumblebee banging a big bass drum. It was Mardis Gras, a week of parades culminating in *Fasnacht*, the German version of Fat Tuesday. The whole procession crowded into this barn-like beer hall at the end of the route where the band leader went around and around, leading the band past four in the morning, musicians falling asleep in the middle of songs, one fellow nodding into his tuba.

A jolly end.

On the appointed day Brad and Ted showed up in the transit lounge with two lovely leather bags, looking relieved to be "home" again. When boarding was called for Chicago they gave the bags to Perry and Carl. Carl grabbed his bag and headed straight for the plane, followed by Perry, the belt of a shapeless houndstooth check overcoat trailing on the ground.

I'd been travelling for over a month and was totally exhausted, dozed on and off the whole way to Chicago and was awoken by the plane touching down. I waited for Perry and Carl to exit, then shadowed them into the international arrivals terminal at O'Hare.

It was around nine in the morning, but the terminal was empty except for our flight. Perry seemed to be breathing a little hard. He looked hung-over, and he'd gotten himself in the wrong line, the one for Alien Arrivals. As my line moved quickly, his dawdled along. I tried to indicate by a series of cartoonish faces that he was in the wrong queue—looked at his line, eyes wide, nostrils flaring, then jerked my head toward my line, nodded and looked back at him, eyebrows raised. He did his best to ignore me.

The agent at the Immigration counter took my passport and declaration form, made some kind of mark and handed them back; and as we stepped into the Customs area our flight was checked by a phalanx of Customs Agents who'd decided to "blitz" the plane, in Customs parlance.

An agent stood me up, led me to a metal table and instructed me to open my suitcase. On top was little Oliver's carving of the *famille de fruits*. Visibly aroused, he began pawing through clothes and probing the suitcase. *Fine, if it meant one less agent to go after the carriers.*

I took a furtive glance around, no sign of Perry or Carl.

"Where did you get these carvings?" the agent asked, looking down at the little bananas and grapes Oliver had carved and polished.

"Africa," I said. "Is that okay with you?"

The agent looked up for a moment, refused the bait and continued unpacking my bags. He turned a mask over and scrutinized the back. Unscrewed a bottle of shampoo. Pretty soon it became clear he hadn't hit the jackpot.

"Ok. Pack these things up," he said and ran off to harass other travelers.

Gathering my stuff I looked up and saw Carl moving smartly along the back of the terminal to an exit. I looked around for Perry but saw nothing, turned slowly to look back at Customs, didn't see him anywhere and concluded he'd made it out safely; and swinging my bag off the table to go, I almost barged right into him as he passed in front of me, head bowed, jacket dragging, escorted by a surly looking Customs Agent into the "Customs shed" in the middle of the floor.

I stood there for a moment watching as the door closed behind him. Then a powerful instinct to flee flooded into every cell of my body, and I hurried outside and got in a cab, sure in my mind and in my gut there was no way for this to end well.

Flight

It was pretty clear that Perry had been arrested. Carl and I had waited for almost two hours in the lobby of the Hyatt, acutely aware that if Perry started talking, we were sitting ducks. So the first thing to do now was to get out of there and check into a new hotel under fake names. This wasn't easy since most hotels required identification. After driving around for an hour in a cab, we finally found some old dive that wasn't asking questions, a twelve story brick affair with a billboard on top of it. The place seemed like it hadn't been remodeled since 1940. I went out to a phone booth and called Alhaji.

To his credit, he remained calm. "Oh, what to do? What to do?" he said, to himself.

In fact, Alhaji was no amateur. He'd worked his way up in crime in the rough and tumble world of Lagos. After getting arrested back in the 80s, he broke out of prison and made his way to Benin, where he became involved in the international side of drug dealing, first in Spain, then eventually taking over the current route, rumor had it from a dead man's wife, a certain Adid.

Outside U.S legal jurisdiction, Alhaji operated several legitimate businesses, burrowing his way at the same time into the government of Republic du Benin. He introduced Claire and me to a supposed cabinet minister. Another time he walked us through security at the airport in Benin, joking that we should open our suitcases for the police, before escorting us right onto the runway where he waved goodbye like someone's auntie on the driveway after Thanksgiving dinner.

Unfortunately, despite his talk of Belgian bank accounts, Swiss Passports and the like, he never really bothered to show us all the ropes. And we, for our part, had no exit strategy whatsoever. Failure and its consequences were just too horrible to contemplate. And so we began a crash course in damage control.

The first order of business was to hand over Carl's bag—even though Perry had been busted, we'd still gotten the other bag through. This involved a game of cat and mouse with a Nigerian couple who came by the hotel room first pretending to have gotten the wrong room, then stopping back several times feigning drunkenness. Then the man came by alone, distraught, looking for his wife. They were actually quite good. Satisfied finally that it was just Carl and me, they came and took the bag and gave us a few thousand dollars. Then the man handed me a cell phone; Alhaji was on the line.

Alhaji wanted us to get to New York to pick up money for legal expenses. Apparently the business of finding a lawyer was up to me. So Carl and I went to his friend's house so he could rent us a car; there was no way in hell we were walking back into that airport or making any kind of credit card transaction.

Carl's friend, Sig, lived in Greektown—a bachelor of indeterminate years, a wisecracking, disbarred Chicago attorney.

At first we tiptoed around the subject, then I saw no reason not to divulge our secret: our guy had probably been arrested with drugs at O'Hare.

"We could get Barney on that," Sig said.

"Right, Barney." Carl said.

"Who the fuck is Barney?" I said

"Barney Hamm. This Lawyer we know," Carl said.

"At least have him find out if they have your friend," Sig said. "You don't want him sitting around in jail; you know, the longer he sits there the more likely he starts talking. You don't think...."

"No. He doesn't know enough. He knows it's not an option. And we'll take care of him."

"So?"

"Yeah, find out. His name is Perry Mays," I said, realizing I was letting things get out of hand—realizing I was acting on the advice of a disbarred attorney ... who came on the recommendation of a mule ... recruited by another mule ... and though they were just supposed to do some preliminary inquiring, it seemed clear that once they got involved the lawyers were going to be hard to get rid of if only because I was dead tired and the more intense things became the more you wanted to close your eyes and block your ears.

Sig drove us to a car rental in town and Carl and I took off to New York. As we fled the city limits, I looked in the rear view mirror. It seemed just a few weeks since I'd driven out here for the first time, Chicago heaving into view like a big stage set.

At some point, overwhelmed by exhaustion, Carl and I pulled into a Motel 6 on route 80 to sleep for a couple of hours. I went into the restaurant to get something to eat. Some traveling salesmen types in cheap, no-iron trousers and plaid jackets were in the bar, drinking. I remember envying them the carelessness of the moment: a bunch of guys in the Midwest getting drunk on a Friday night, far from the daily responsibility of their lives. I ordered a scotch and soda and took a swallow, but I just wanted to cry.

Early next morning Carl and I drove to Cleveland Airport, caught a flight to JFK, rented a car and drove to a midtown Holiday Inn. In the meantime, the lawyers in Chicago had found out that Perry was being held on charges of importation of a controlled substance. I called Alhaji. An hour later there was a knock on the door; a Nigerian courier had $40,000 for us.

The lawyers in Chicago seemed interested in taking the case. There was a bond hearing for Perry the next day. Hamm wanted to know what kind of money we could come up with. I told him the money was no problem. He said he'd be willing to represent us for around $30,000. While I didn't know anything about this guy, it beat looking for lawyers in the phone book. Plus he seemed hip to the facts and seemed willing to represent our interests. And time was ticking.

That night Hamm called and said bond had been set for $100,000. Ten would get Perry out. So next morning I went out to wire the bail money plus a retainer. I walked out of the hotel and across the street. The rental car was gone. The sign on the street said No parking 6am-8am. *Fuck.* They had the car at an impound lot on Pier 76 off of West Side Drive. On the cab ride over, I told the cabbie "Turn here." The cabbie for some inexplicable reason turned to me to say, "where?" promptly slamming into the car stopped at the light in front of him.

I got out of the cab and walked around to the front of the car where the driver, a North African, was looking wildly at the crumpled hood. Something didn't feel right. I pressed my fingers together at the tip of my nose and pulled. There was a cracking sound of bone and cartilage going back into place. The cabbie gestured for me to stay as he argued with the other driver. I threw a twenty on his seat and ran through traffic. At the impound lot they asked for the rental agreement. So I ran back across the highway to a copy shop and called the rental agency and had them fax the agreement— then ran back to the lot, got the car, returned it and wired the money to the attorneys from a Western Union; they had me send the money to an alias and then call with the confirmation number so they could collect it incognito. Then I left a few thousand dollars with Carl and flew home to see my poor sweetheart, L.

We'd achieved a tenuous détente, saw one another occasionally, most often to drop off my car, which served as a lifeline of sorts. I'd promised her it was all over. I was getting out…. Now someone had been arrested. It was unfinished business that had to be concluded. Things needed to be seen through. If everything got taken care of like it was supposed to, I might yet find my way out of this. I had to get back to Chicago and meet with the lawyers. There was no mincing words or sneaking around now.

Crash

Our dumb mule Perry sat there in the conference room of Barney Hamm's law office like the prodigal son as we surged round him slapping him on the back. He'd stayed two nights in Chicago Metropolitan Correction Center, a federal jail in the south Loop. Now he was enjoining us to "close ranks"—kind of a strange choice of words I thought much later, though at the time it hardly registered.

"You know all your legal expenses will be taken care of," I said. "We can beat this case."

Everyone looked at Barney. "This is my partner, Jon Gull," Hamm said, nodding at Gull.

Ham & Gull, I murmured....

Gull stood up, wavy hair, Armani suit and sneer on his face.

"Even if drugs *were* found in the bag Perry was carrying, we can make a case that he had the wrong bag—and I believe that's true

... that's true ... because I would never accept this case knowing that illicit funds were being used," Gull joked, insulating himself with lawyerly care.

At length he concluded, "and that is really our only choice, other than taking a plea, which is something the prosecution only offers when they see you're serious about trial."

Gull was laying it out just the way we wanted him to. The way anyone guilty as sin would want him to.

"Of course they're going to try to get you to cooperate," he said to Perry. "To name names. If you do this we can't work with you. That's just admitting guilt. And they're just going to use you. Guys who start cooperating get into a never-ending relationship with the government, and they wind up getting the same kind of time if they took a plea. So I don't think we need to say any more about *that*."

Bravo, I thought. Things were actually starting to look up.

After the meeting, I had lunch with Barney Hamm at Italian Village. We went downstairs to the cantina to a booth in the corner of the room. The place was empty except for a couple old-timers watching the Blackhawks game at the bar.

"You shoulda seen that guy Perry at MCC," Hamm said, referring to the Metropolitan Correctional Center, the federal jail in Chicago. "Not very polished."

"Yeah. I only met him once."

"He looked like a farmer in those orange overalls."

What's going to happen?" I said.

"We start rehearsing for trial. You give us some money to hold onto for Perry, for spending; we'll dole it out, a few thousand a month. And make sure nobody talks on the phone. If he needs to talk, you meet here."

"What happens at trial?"

"We establish he's a respectable citizen. College graduate, job, family."

Perry was a little deficient in that area.

"I don't really know the guy."

"He told me his last job was a fucking Mary Kay salesman," Hamm said, guffawing. "Can you picture that hick driving around in a pink Cadillac?"

I wasn't quite enjoying the levity. "Can we win?"

"Fifty-fifty."

I sat there in stunned silence. I knew what "fifty-fifty" meant, and yet I'd allowed myself to hope recklessly. "What?" I croaked.

"Well," Hamm said, clearly enjoying himself, "the time to be scared was before you brought heroin onto a plane."

After lunch I was all too happy to go straight to the airport and fly home. Back in Provincetown I continued to work on the magazine, drink copious amounts of alcohol and generally make a bad job of holding a relationship together. L was doing environmental ed.—hiking across salt marshes trailed by children swishing butterfly nets; lecturing adults on dragonfly reproduction; reading Henry Beston by lamplight at night as moths fluttered against the screen.

What she actually thought about my recent developments, if she thought about them at all, I couldn't say. It's possible the menace that overshadowed me was too abstract to imagine; or I'd minimized it to a point that she simply discounted it. And we muddled through with a good deal of ambivalence between us, and things unsaid, like unexploded mines overgrown with weeds.

Mid-summer arrived, but it felt as if I'd lost a sense of taste or smell. Peter and I managed to put together a couple more issues of the magazine and threw a big release party—L drove into town wearing a little black cocktail dress and we sipped martinis and smoked cigarettes like in the old days…. But the whole time it felt as if I was smiling through a thin film that separated me from everyone else. And despite my daily rounds of coffee shops, wharves, bars, galleries and restaurants, I plodded to and from my apartment each day as mechanically as a pile of parts wired together.

I was sitting out the heat of a late Saturday morning. The telephone rang. An unfamiliar voice on the other end began to speak. (How I hated the tyranny of the telephone, from which any stranger might waylay you.)

"Is this Nicholas Fillmore?" the voice said.

"Yes." I said.

"This is Cape Cod Hospital...."

I trembled, and the receiver leapt out of my hand.

"Your girlfriend was in a car accident."

"She's okay," the nurse hastened to add, though in the intervening seconds I found myself plummeting through a void.... (Strictly an afterthought, it occurs to me that the "simple perfect" would have been the more cogent verb tense.)

L was sitting on the edge of a gurney at the back of the nurse's station—I could pick the lovely tilt of her face out of a crowd—looking toward the door when I walked in. She started to stand, then grasped her hip in pain as I rushed to her side.

She was dressed in a paper gown, looking terribly tired.

"I'm sorry about the car," she said, bursting into tears.

Oh, my darling, my love, my life, my L....

"Are you okay?"

"I think so. They think so."

"Does it hurt?"

She nodded, the tears welling. "It was so loud."

I held her in my arms, alarmed by unfamiliar, antiseptic smells.

Very gingerly we put her clothes on and drove back to her place.

That night I slept at the foot of her bed, listening to her breathing. In the morning we went to the salvage yard where the

Granada lay vanquished, its heavy steel frame bent from a passenger-side collision.

"You'd have been killed if you were in the car." She started to cry.

"I wasn't."

"You could have been."

"But...."

"I'm sorry," she said.

"I'm sorry. I'm sorry. I'm sorry," I said....

It would be pat to say the accident fixed everything. It didn't. The same old restlessness that drove me hither and thither soon began twitching in all my joints again. Not to mention Perry Mayes was in Chicago possessed of his deadly secret.

Entropy

As Perry's case wore on, status hearing after inconclusive status hearing, it soon became clear that none of the principles had any interest in resolving matters right away; to the contrary, the longer they were able to draw things out, the more things accrued to their self-interest: the feds in dragging a confession out of Perry (assuming they hadn't already and weren't just using him to draw out everyone else), the defense attorneys in billing another month's fees. In fact, the lawyers had started asking for more money, explaining for one reason or another that a motion for speedy trial would be of no avail. Then Perry started asking for more money. Then the Goddamn Professionals started complaining.

I took another trip to Paris to pick up money. In Chicago the lawyers dropped a bombshell; they wanted more money, $10,000 a month or something crazy like that. Alhaji laughed. He said to tell the lawyers they could have a bonus if they got Perry off. The lawyers bristled as if I'd trod upon some delicate loafer of feeling. Then on the eve of a status hearing Barney Hamm called to say if they didn't receive x dollars by x date, they'd quit the case, and if Perry didn't have representation at the hearing, the judge would revoke his bond—which was entirely untrue, of course, but what did I know?

At the last minute I got Alhaji to release more money, which Ted went to Paris to pick up. In the process of passing it to the lawyers a couple thousand went missing, and my feelings of loyalty began to suffer a severe strain. Of course the payment was only a stop-gap, and the whole situation replayed itself in a matter of months.

Finally Gull said that he was "disinclined" to represent Perry any further and that I owed him money. You could just hear him sneering through the line. In no position to report anyone to the bar for ethics violations, I told him that our business was concluded and hung up.

Perry hired new lawyers, and I paid a retainer. Nothing happened for a couple months. Then the calls from Perry started.

"I don't have any money," he whined.

"Look, man, nobody has any money right now. Get a job."

"You said I'd be taken care of."

"I said expenses would be taken care of."

"You said if anybody ever got caught…."

"I don't know anything about anybody getting *caught*," I said quickly. This was getting a little explicit, and I cut off the conversation before he could draw me out any further. "Who gave you this number? Did Brad give you this number? You get in touch with me through Brad. You call here again and we're through," I said, shaking.…

About this time Claire called. She'd had a courier pinched in San Francisco, a friend of her sister's.

I laughed. After scolding me for pushing a trip through, she'd done the same thing, but instead of routing the heroin through Europe, she'd tried to bring it straight from the Philippines. It was like Russian roulette with her since Temper left.

When the recruiting house in the Mission or whatever-the-fuck turned out to be a mirage, and the sex became routine, and the champagne went flat, Temper had spun on the heels of her Doc Martens and gone merrily back to some appropriately-urbane post-college existence, certain she'd left the whole mess behind her, and Claire began recycling couriers, some terrier instinct unable to let go the bone.

With our mounting legal problems, the only thing left for us to do was arrange a final trip to Benin to beg for money.

After flying into Togo we rented a car and drove along the coast. It was bittersweet seeing it all end like this, and I tried to take everything in: the smell of cook fires, sun flashing in the palms, time slowing with the sway of women's hips along the roadside, heavy loads balanced atop their heads.

You could run away here. I pictured myself set up in some line or other, a house and car—a rich man by African standards—consumed by whiskey and beautiful, long-legged African women and nostalgia for home.

As the road from Lomé to Cotonou sank into shadows, I tried not to think that Claire and I might easily find ourselves legal adversaries; tried not to think that we *were* in fact legal adversaries—that in going our separate ways we'd merely doubled our risk.

Of course some very similar thought occurred to Alhaji, who made us wait at the Cotonou Sheraton for several days.

Claire and I drank beers at a little café by the hotel pool. Africans and Europeans reclined on lounge chairs in stylish metallic swimwear and white terrycloth robes. A German engineer splashed in a wading pool with his kids. A bell rang and a porter in pillbox hat paraded about the patio holding up a sign on a stick: telephone call for a Messr. Such-and-such. An air of colonial peace and civility prevailed.

Beyond the manicured lawn, a wavering chain link fence with a gap cut out and a windbreak of ironwoods was a gritty beach. The sound of distant drumming tore past on the wind. A sign warned of dangerous currents. And the black silhouette of a Nigerian oil tanker slid past far out in the Bight.

A couple White guys in suits eyed us from the security stand.

"Who are those guys?" I asked the bartender.

"Those are the cops, man."

"What are the cops doing here?" I asked.

Claire shook her head.

There was some relevant piece of information I couldn't remember. Something that Claire had said once kept trying to pop into my head....

The next day Benin President Soglo's motorcade pulled up to the hotel. I wandered down to have a look. Alhaji passed right in front of me. I started to open my mouth but realized he was ignoring me, so I clamped it shut and went into a store to buy cigarettes, then went up to the room. Finally he called and had a driver take us to his new house, a white, concrete structure along Moorish lines on the lot behind the old house.

We went in through a sliding glass door at the side and were served lunch. Alhaji came downstairs for a moment then excused himself and disappeared upstairs again with his ruined stomach.

After lunch he came back down and showed us to some expensive-looking leather couches. As I went towards a chair I bashed my shin into a low glass coffee table, which seemed to take up all the space in the middle of the seating arrangement. The thing momentarily caught my attention: a thick slab of beveled glass with crossed glass golf clubs adorning the underside. Alhaji looked down at it almost apologetically. For a second it seemed he was going to have it removed.

Then he started to talk. He spoke impressionistically, running on to people and incidents I only had a vague acquaintance with. Then bits and pieces would come out directed at you. And I realized that as much as we held him in awe, he feared us—feared our Whiteness in a way we could not have guessed. Then some kind of anger flared in him.

"You can not be a man, Nicky, if you talk about people. You cannot. Maybe you do. And one day you will become sick."

He knew, even if we didn't yet.

"I always told you people, I will be with you. Maybe after you take care of your problem we can do business."

Finally we had our say. We needed money. Our people needed money. The lawyers needed money.

"The lawyers should give you *back* money," he told me. Then he said Binga would deliver us 10,000 in Lomé, back in Togo. A pittance. Then he sent us away.

After all the intervening years I understand Alhaji perfectly well. Though not without human feeling, he was a creature of mammon. (We, on the other hand, were fucking amateurs.)

This was business only. I realized it once when in a moment of candor I'd asked him why we couldn't get involved in diamonds, anything else.

"There is just too much money in the heroin, Nicky." It was the one time I ever heard him use the word *heroin*.

No, there was too much money to fool around with diamonds. Or dilettantes. Or to let friendship stand in the way. And so it was out of friendship that he sent us away, though we couldn't have understood it in our present needy condition.

Home Invasion

As we got off the plane in New York someone was checking ID's right outside the door. I saw my name on a short list on a clipboard the agent was holding. He asked some routine questions: where I'd come from, what I was doing, hesitating like there was something else he wanted to ask.

After the interview, I fast-walked off the jet bridge and jogged down a short hallway to the main lobby. An immigration counter was opening to the far right and I skipped over, showed my papers and hustled out to the street, leaving a couple agents prepared to do a follow-up interview empty-handed. Claire stood in line at immigration. An agent came walking back, shrugging his shoulders. Later, she told me they just waved her through.

At the domestic air terminal I caught a flight to Hartford. An hour later, my parents drove the car the short distance home.

I'd made fun of them for driving to the wrong arrivals gate when I should have thanked them for the great constancy of their lives. No matter what frivolous lark I flew on, they were always there when it came time to bail. Whatever excess I indulged in, they patiently forbore.

"Guess where I was."

"Where?"

"Africa." This cracked me up because my father always said "Africa" when you asked too many questions: "Where are we going, Dad?" "Africa," he'd say. "Where were you, Dad?" "Africa."

"Oh?" my mother said.

I'd mentioned Africa before. Just now it all seemed slightly ridiculous, completely passé; I wasn't even connected any longer. So I made a very cursory account of my trip and changed the subject. It was a necessary skill I'd learned.

We talked about the neighbors and the changes to town, which seemed to be accelerating. My own childhood was still something recognizable to my parents. I'd grown up in the same place they had: played on the same ball fields and worked in the same tobacco fields—down on my arse under nets in wet rows of tobacco, picking and piling leaves ... and dreaming of the great world beyond, as they had: my mother of joining the ballet, my father for two years in the Marines.

They found the material of their lives early on. On construction sites in Hartford working alongside grown men at fifteen and swimming on the Connecticut River after work, out where the main current swept dark and cold under your feet, spinning you around, my father had found an existence strong enough to satisfy him. Whatever I found wasn't enough, and when I was old enough one year I left and never returned really....

My parent's house, a 50s-built Cape with a barn-like addition, was the romance of our lives. From the front yard I'd watched my father nailing rafters high overhead as the last daylight disappeared from the sky. My mother decorated it in antiques, gay as a robin flying from branch to branch with a bit of colored ribbon. It was the room we gathered in, the room we grew up in, the room in which I have the last living memory of my grandfather and grandmother, whom I sense more deeply each year in the expression of my genes.

The first Christmas the addition was built, my father moved the little "tea wagon" my two sisters and my parents and I ate at (sometimes the wheel would fall off, and my dad would dive under the table cursing as our plates slid around on top). Then he cut a hole in the kitchen wall and we stepped into the new space, all pink insulation like the inside of some great shell. We built a fire and brought the Christmas tree in, and my father, in his day a physical presence on the basketball court, leaped high in the air and lightly slapped one of the exposed ties, a 30-footer, which vibrated back and forth a half-dozen times before the outward thrust of the rafters pulled it taut again.

After we drove home from the airport, we had dinner. My parents, as was their habit, drifted off to different parts of the house. Late that night I found my mother working in her basement studio.

She was stenciling a black tin pot. My mother was a member of The Historical Society of Early American Decoration, and Master Craftsman. From time to time she travelled to Western Pennsylvania or Williamsburg to learn some esoteric brushstroke: how to simulate wood grain with a bird feather; then she'd return home to teach classes each night of the week—some painterly, some raucous smoke-filled affairs—before escaping back into her solitude, where she felt most comfortable, in the stillness of late night amid loops and scrolls: little tendrils of gold leaf encircling a strawberry.

Whenever I came home to visit, this is where I would talk to my mother, who believed in candor in all things.

"Are you heading back to the Cape tomorrow?" she asked.

Of course. Impatient as always to escape back into my own late night.

"I saw your friend Jimmy the other day at the supermarket," my mother said.

—Jimmy who stole submarines and whose mother taught CCD. "Oh, yeah? What's he up to?" I couldn't imagine spending my whole life in the same place—to persevere without even the illusion of reinventing oneself every few years.

"Well, his parents had to get a restraining order against him...."

"Egad," I said.

"He hit his father."

"What did they raise the rent or something?"

My mother laughed.

"Hey, Mom..." an old memory jogged free, "do you remember that orange submarine?"

"You mean the one you guys took from the birthday party and I had to slap you around the back yard to get the truth out of you?"

"Yeah, that one...."

"What about it?"

"Eh, nothing."

This was all just prelude to the real talk and work of family history—of the great Aunts and Uncles from the two sides of my mother's family, the Russian Poles and the Polish Poles, the Pytors and the Stanislaws ... undertaken to glimpse some essential, genetic explanation of ourselves.

In the end all roads led back to the farm, that spiritual center. There seemed to be a moment in the forties, after the War, when my mother was just a tiny little girl with blonde hair, and she was the apple of her daddy's eye and he was the apple of hers, when the world seemed a perfect thing—a summer morning hanging out the wash with her mother, birds singing in the woods beyond the field…. The bottle in the cupboard, the cap screwed tight…. The tragedy of our lives is not its flaws, but the longing for some perfection held briefly in our hands.

"If I needed to keep some things with you, could I do that?"

"Like what?" Mom asked.

"Things. Money."

"Of course. Why?"

"… I was just wondering."

In bed that evening, the scene at JFK came flooding back, then a deep longing for childhood: the safety of that bed by the north-facing window, knowing that whatever transpired during the day I could pull the covers over my head at night and let sweet sleep come.

Over the next months, Claire and I each went increasingly broke. Claire sold her Miata. I moved into a studio apartment and ran up credit card debt. At some point Claire called with a proposition. She needed some things removed from her house. By somebody else. So one Saturday I got up early and drove out route 6 to the Mass Pike and up 91 in autumnal sunshine and a blaze of colors. At the appointed time I pulled up to the house, parked in the driveway and slipped through the side door, which she'd left unlocked. It was a little jewel box, all lined in polished wood and fieldstone.

I peered out the windows at the neighbors' houses.

Home invasion was a whole different frisson than drug smuggling. I'd never liked stealing, even as a little kid when all my little friends started stealing penny candy. You kept looking over your shoulder expecting someone's hand on your arm.

Yet everything seemed so peaceful on this Saturday morning in southern Vermont. Straw-colored light streaked through red and gold leaves against a hard blue sky. I had a sudden urge to make coffee and sit out on the porch with a book.

I picked up Claire's Waterman pen and set it back on the desk, then unplugged some things and threw them in the back of my car and drove away.

Claire vanished for a few months after that; then she called. Her lawyer had some vague misgivings about Claire's mule who'd been busted in San Francisco. There were whisperings about a superseding indictment. Some unseen force was massing on the horizon.

We met in Boston to talk freely. Claire, practically hysterical with fear, spoke in incomprehensible code. "Papa won't talk to the boy's lawyers," she said.

"Who? Alhaji?"

"Don't use names" she said.

"What?"

"Don't say names."

"You want to be careful now?"

"If you keep talking like that I'll have to leave," she said.

"Look, you have your problem, I have mine."

She shook her head and something mean and low that wanted to strike out and cause pain stirred down inside me.

"Well, you should have thought about that before you brought heroin onto a plane."

Her face went bright with alarm and she put on her coat. I followed her outside, and we stood in harsh winter light on the top of Boylston St. on a dead Sunday afternoon in Boston.

"Fucking great."

Who knows if we said goodbye or not, but it felt like goodbye as Claire hurriedly walked down the street and disappeared around a corner.

Of course it would be disingenuous to blame Claire in any way for my own choices, but now she'd made herself unavailable—as had Alhaji.

How much of our operation revolved around her emotional and financial needs? Whatever you were feeling, whatever you wanted, she always seemed to delve a yard deeper.

Then it came to me what she'd said back in Northampton when she was recruiting me: she said in the end we could always rat.

At this point another Provincetown winter was going to break me. I'd kept my half of the money Alhaji gave us and had some credit left on my cards, but I needed to make money. I needed to rejoin the world, if only temporarily. There just wasn't enough momentum to get where I was going.

An End to the Affair

In New York I took a studio in the West Village near the Meat-packing District and found work in the composing room of an old publishing house in Penn Plaza, walking to and from work every day twenty-some blocks up Eighth Avenue, persuading myself all the while that I was living a normal life, even as the hand of reckoning closed around my throat.

On Fridays I had enough money after bills to buy a bag of rice, a half dozen cans of black beans, some vitamins and a gallon of bourbon. The rest was tip money for the angelic barmaids who poured drink after drink for the pleasure of my beery company.

After sticking with me through all my misadventures, L had moved to Hawaii to do field research, leaving me to work out Act II for myself. I'd walked her down to the 14th St. subway stop, en route to JFK.

"I'll see you when you get back," I said.

She nodded.

"I love you."

A sob escaped her lips....

And she was gone.

I sat there now before the bottles and mirrors swallowing a regret lodged in my throat.

They'd scheduled me for second shift at work, which allowed me to drink till closing. Each night I found myself drifting across town into the east village, lower Broadway, Alphabet City and back to Union Square, reveling in an objectless longing for the rhythm of traffic lights blinking into the distance. A feeling of eternity in the frigid night air.

One night when I came home from work, there were a couple cruisers with lights flashing in front of the apartment building. Screwing up my courage I approached a cop. "What's up?"

"Some guy died inside."

In the apartment right above mine, maybe four and a half feet above my bed-loft, a house sitter had suffered a fatal heart attack and remained undiscovered until the fermentation of bodily humors wafted into the hall, alerting neighbors. How many days and nights had he lain there?

I'd gotten my position at the publishing company after the shop foreman suffered a massive coronary right in the composing room. My fellow compositors were still spooked. The fellow's presence hung in the air.

Some nights I went drinking at the Village Idiot on 14th, a couple blocks from my apartment. Fueled by $1.25 PBRs and Hank Williams, my mind unreeled in the tall shadows on the ceiling above the bar, the only company a big tank in the front window with an alternating cast of turtles you could feed goldfish to, three for a dollar.

There was an odd sex club across the street. A tall, dark dominatrix—drag queen, doubtless—was coming out. Inside, there didn't appear to actually be any sex going on. Some guy was strapped to a gurney, looking like he'd been through some kind of rigors. A couple groups of people moved around the room to other stations, swirling ice in their glasses. It was like being in an art gallery in a way. I finished my drink and dashed back out to the street.

One time this guy persuaded me after many beers to deliver newspapers with him on his route up in Harlem. He told me I would see New York, in early morning light, as few had seen it. Spuyten Duyvil and other place names that are like poetry to a New Yorker. So we took a Path Train to New Jersey, walked across a field and into the garage of *The Daily News*. As we signed in for a delivery truck, he nodded towards some guys at a table. "Mob. That one," he said, "is waiting to go to prison. Don't look."

I thought about calling Alhaji. I could orchestrate another run, I convinced myself, despite the likelihood the Feds were watching me. Call Alhaji at his office and he'd have someone give me a number. Use new couriers.

Or I could pay Perry Mayes a visit.

Of course I was too scared to do any such thing. And if I imagined that I was still in the game and continued to mention "overseas business" to random acquaintances, friends of friends, strangers, I did this knowing that it really was all over.

In the end, I'd done what I could. There was just one more thing.

We were still trying to get *Squid* magazine going again. In fact, we had enough regular advertisers to support publication. Pete had some articles. I was working on some things from a New York angle, hoping the Provincetown-New York perspective would fly. The transvestite prostitutes who cruised the Meatpacking District was probably not the best idea.

One night, I prevailed upon one of these creatures of the night to come to my place for an interview. After convincing her I did *not* want the blowjob, and asking a few preliminary question, I had a little bout of nausea and hurried into the bathroom. When I returned, my interview subject was making off with a CD Walkman and a brief struggle ensued. You'd think being caught in the act would be enough to put an end to the affair, but I suppose leaning into darkened cars exiting West Side Drive must endow one with an indomitability of spirit. She wouldn't give up. Finally the prospect of being found by neighbors wrestling an Amazonian transvestite in acid green tights and patent leather knee boots in the hallway kind of dampened my fight, and *I let the thing go.*

… Another time, I stole a gross of eggs off a loading dock around the corner from my apartment. Back home I made a batch of fried eggs and wolfed them down. Then I made scrambled eggs, poached eggs, eggs with tomato sauce. Finally I hard-boiled them all to keep them from going bad. I ate so many eggs that for a week my farts smelled like eggs.

I was ready to go now.

Arrest

Broken threads of sleep wavered overhead. Familiar sounds filtered into my brain. Then a heavy pounding on the door jolted me upright.

They're here.

"Who is it?" I said, conscious of a note of hysteria forcing its way into my voice.

"Police," they said.

"Who?" I said, stalling for time.

"Police."

I scrambled down from my loft and pulled on pants and a shirt from the night before, cracked the door and peered out. Somebody was shoving credentials in my face. I undid the safety chain and stepped into the hall.

Three agents and a couple uniforms were crowded on the mat.

"Can I help you?"

"Do you recognize this man?" they asked, handing over a tattered sepia photo of ... *Che Guevara?*

Oh God. "No. No, I don't recognize him," I said, hopefully.

"Mr. Fillmore?" they persisted.

"Yes."

"... Agents from Chicago, Illinois," they said, their voices coming in static bursts, "... for conspiracy to import a controlled substance. You have the right...."

The apartment door behind me threatened to close and suddenly it seemed very important that we not get locked out of my apartment—that we do this in an orderly fashion. *Just a little more time, please.*

"Let me get the key." Back inside the apartment, I whisked the key off a table and stuck it in my pocket. This sudden movement caught them off guard. Somebody shoved me against the wall and there was frantic yelling and there might even have been guns drawn, but I couldn't tell because everything closed in ... a kind of blackout.

"Ok, Ok," I said.

"Ok," they said. "Ok."

This was my initiation into the criminal justice system, the rough equivalent of a fraternity hazing, except at the end of the night they didn't clap you on the back and straighten your tie and say, "Welcome, brother." Instead, you know, they hauled you off to Gowanus Bay.

One of the agents led me into the apartment.

"Have a seat," he said.

There was a stool in the middle of the room. The agents closed the door and stood in front of me. For a moment nobody said anything; we just looked at each other. Customs Agent Wayne was a tall, delicate-boned fellow, a look of torment on his face.

D.E.A. Agent Brett was shorter, squarer jawed, an ironic smirk that said, *Don't let this guy fool you.* They were both dressed in jeans, fleece jackets, hiking shoes, sports watches, young guys in their early thirties. A third guy from the New York Customs office stood in the background fiddling with stuff on my bookshelves. The uniforms stayed in the hallway.

"We know about Mickey."

"And Hester," they said.

Hearing them banter names about in this airy way put me in a bad mood. *How could they know about Mickey and Hester? I'd only met Mickey once, on my first trip to Chicago when we smoked heroin and watched Star Trek together; and Hester had simply vanished in a puff of smoke after Claire and I took over.*

Perry—our guy who'd been caught in O'Hare—didn't know *either of these people at all. Maybe somebody had blabbed to him about Hester, who was not without her fag-hag charms....*

Did I have any weapons?

"A kitchen knife over on the counter," I said, seized by an impulse to be helpful.

"Forget that. Is that a safe under your desk?"

"Yes."

"Is there any money in it?"

Once there was money. Now there was nothing. Just the dirty, sweet smell. And the agents' chagrin at finding nothing made me feel a little better, if that's what this was all about, in the end: money.

"We know about the lost bag," they said, pressing their opening gambit.

So?

"We know about the trips to Africa. We know about Alhaji."

So? They knew about Alhaji. My mind raced, engaging in a superfluous calculus. *Could the Goddamn Professionals, Brad and Ted, have been so careless? Or was something else going on here?*

"We know about the exchange in Zurich."

If it was Brad and Ted—but it couldn't be them—if they were cooperating, then I was totally fucked; they probably had me on tape talking about Perry. How long had this been going on for? Had they all been cooperating from the start?

"We can help you if you help us. But there's a line of people. We need to get your statement."

The idea that my information was redundant had me panicked. They knew enough, I was sure, to make a case. Of course you weren't supposed to say anything now. This was where you were supposed to say you wanted to talk to a lawyer.

"Ok," I said. "You got me."

"We don't have Claire."

I gave them her address. They made a call and I imagined with a mixture of dread and satisfaction the agents closing in on the carriage house in Vermont, the same thing here being replayed up north. (Actually, they pulled an old chestnut out of the Marshals' playbook and nabbed her in a fast food drive-through I think, poor thing.)

They wanted me to get Alhaji on the phone. Agent Wayne plugged a pickup into a mini tape recorder. I stuck the earpiece in my ear and dialed the number, the old pattern locked away in my brain. And as Alhaji came on the line my heart sank. The last two years was just another in a succession of pretenses. There was no graceful way out now, just the indignity of naming names.

Of course Alhaji was possessed of a preternatural sense. "I want you to call me back in a day or two. I will give you a new number." Then the line disconnected.

We were done here.

I was sitting in a chair surrounded by agents. I wanted to get up to look for a cigarette. I wanted to use the toilet, to go down to the corner for a cup of coffee. Walk up Eighth Ave. and smell the warm spring air coming off the Hudson. Not today. Not any time soon.

Every Moment You Are Passing from Freedom

They led me out of my apartment in handcuffs, right on the street, the neighbors talking to the cops on the stoop, cabs and bike messengers going by, the sound of delivery trucks, life going on.

Did the cuffs show under my shirtsleeves? I wondered, alarmed. And suddenly it seemed very important that we get the basic arrest right. No take-down in the street. No segment on the 5 o'clock news. A civilized walk around the corner to a waiting car. (Solzhenitsyn says something like this in his *Gulag Archipelago*.)

Before taking me to jail, the agents brought me to a downtown Customs office. Although we went through a basement sally port, the office itself didn't seem especially secure. Maybe a locked door or two. One last chance to bolt. For the next four years I'd be housed in a maximum-security administrative facility, 15 floors up, behind reinforced concrete and iron grating.

The agents were searching for the ink pad to fingerprint me. I looked at the doorknob, and an immense exhaustion came over me. All I could do was smile meekly and answer their questions, curious in some weird way where this would all lead.

At length they drove me to Brooklyn Metropolitan Detention Center, the Manhattan skyline dropping from sight as we crossed over the East River; and as they delivered me to the front door of the jail, an old postal sorting station all wire mesh and battleship grey inside, I was sad to see Agents Brett and Wayne go, the last connections to my recent, real life.

There were four other guys in the holding cell, a small room just inside the front door of the prison, almost cozy in its way. Two younger guys were fast asleep, turtled inside their sweatshirts. Two older guys talked between themselves in hushed tones so as not to alarm the others. As I listened to their conversation, their situation began to illuminate my own.

"We're looking at mad time," one fellow said to the other, in earnest. And then he said it again. "We're looking at *mad* time."

You could imagine, almost, the terror that would drive an animal to gnaw its own limb off.

The agony ground on for another three, four hours, possibly more, before life began to stir in the hallway and the jailers came to process us.

After being strip-searched, fitted with prison khakis and canvas slippers, fingerprinted and photo-i.d.'d, we were sent up to the unit, a big, open dorm with rows of metal bunk beds and an adjoining rec area. The rec. area looked onto a large air shaft around which other units were clustered. A rowdy throng of bodies surged against the fence, yelling and gesticulating to co-defendants on other floors, a bright blue square of sky burning above it all.

Someone must have led me to a bunk, I honestly don't remember. It was 1996 and the Yankees were on the verge of renewed greatness. A lot of guys were watching a television bolted to the ceiling. Paul O'Neill was at bat. An Italian fellow was exhorting his team; this was going to be the year.

I watched for an inning, then threw a sheet over a piss-stained mattress, pulled an army blanket over my head and slept.

Next morning I actually felt a momentary elation, as if thankful to find myself alive and in one piece, so dark was the broadcast from my psyche. By degrees my situation filtered into conscious understanding. I was faced with the grim task of making telephone calls.

A line formed against a wall, so I walked over and stood behind the last guy. The fellow in charge came briskly over to get me in the line for the "White phone." (Prison has its rules, existing like all revealed truths in an amber of self-proof. But I didn't know any of this stuff yet.)

My mother answered the phone. "Can I talk to dad?" I said.

My father came on the line, and my heart broke.

On the morning of my arraignment, the Marshalls drove me to the federal courthouse in Manhattan. I met an attorney in a little conference room. His immediate concern was damage control.

"The prosecutors in Chicago are talking about thirty years to life," he said. "I don't think you should tell your father." My father, who'd hired the attorney, had driven down from Connecticut and was sitting in the courtroom.

"No," I said, though it seemed to me his concern was misplaced. "I need to get to Chicago is all."

Courtroom 5A was a scale model of ones they hold trial in: blonde wainscoting with copious trim, paneling inscribed with some Latin verses. The dock was sunk into the floor so you felt like you were in some kind of arena—which you were. Above it all in hallucinatory grandeur sat the judge, an ornament atop a wedding cake.

"In the case of The United States of America versus Nicholas Fillmore, Jr., you have been charged with engaging in a criminal conspiracy to import a controlled substance," the judge intoned. "How do you plead?"

"Not guilty," my lawyer whispered."

"Not guilty, your honor."

"Do you want a hearing to determine bond?"

"No, sir."

"No?"

The lawyer had conveyed to me that the prosecutors in Chicago did not recommend bond. Loathe to antagonize them in any way, I declined. "No, sir."

"Do you want to contest extradition?"

"No, sir."

"Let the record show defendant has waived the right to a bond hearing and waived the right to an extradition proceeding. Therefore I transfer defendant Nicholas Fillmore to custody of the United States Marshals Service," he said, glancing down to check his lines, "for extradition to the Seventh Circuit Court of Northern Illinois."

A couple of Marshalls stepped forward and began moving me toward the exit. I turned back toward the gallery. My dad had stood up. Desperate, not knowing what else to do, I gave an unconvincing thumbs-up. Then they took me inside.

Con Air

A week later they packed me out of Brooklyn MDC and drove me to Stewart Airport, just south of Poughkeepsie. On the back side of the airport was a military installation, gray unmarked 747 surrounded by a litter of vans, various law enforcement busily uncuffing and cuffing prisoners. Four U.S. Marshals kept a perimeter guard, three with M16s, one in a brown duster with shotgun thrown over his shoulder, no kidding.

A light spring rain fell in the surrounding hills as Marshalls finished shackling prisoners about the wrists and ankles. And there was a long moment everyone seemed to forget what he was doing, the Marshalls sipping steaming coffee from Styrofoam cups, the prisoners nodding in place. It was a reprieve, a last glance of light and shadow as one crossed over, thinking of loved ones left behind.—

I'd scrambled to get word to L, who was due back from Hawaii. I'd called my best friend in New York, had him call her best friend in San Francisco, where L would be stopping off, and break the news: "Nick in Jail. Apartment crime scene. Stay away."

Dreadful. Dreadful, I murmured, a last gasp in the middle of the river as the water came up to my chin....

Then someone spoke or rattled their keys ... and the spell was broken.

The Marshals had a uniformly gray appearance, as if they had been out in the weather for a long time.

"Where we headed?" I asked, surprised at my own forwardness, fairly certain I was violating some kind of etiquette.

"Oklahoma. Land of the free, home of the brave," a Marshall with deep creases in his neck answered. It seemed to me that he was over-doing it just a little, but it made sense, looking at all the cowboy mouths and bandy legs.

A Marshall with a passenger list nervously paced back and forth till they'd finally got us lined up to their liking. Then they marched us up boarding stairs into the plane and sat us down in order. The fellow next to me, a mustachioed Mexican, bent forward as in prayer (or crash position) trying to eat peanut butter crackers out of his lap. The surprising thing was everyone *looked* like a convict, even those guys who, like me, had been re-issued their street clothes.

Anyway, it was like getting into wet clothes all over again. And when we arrived in Oklahoma City, we were soon enough divested of our remaining worldly possessions. I donated my Doc Martens, black jeans and shirt to local charity.

"That, too," a guard said, and I worked a silver ring L made off my finger and dropped it into a manila envelope.

The plane had taxied right up to the prison like some mother ship and disgorged us. Then they marched us en masse, swaggering and shuffling, down a long, low, thickly-painted concrete corridor to several holding cells—three sides concrete block, one side wire mesh, thankfully—where we stood around, too crowded to do much else, for several hours. Then they put us through the usual reception: strip search, prison issue, photo i.d., and sent us to our unit clutching a blanket and towel.

I shuffled from the strip search to the next station, where a mild-looking Corrections Officer was handing out underwear. He reached into a big gray bin and pulled out an enormous pair of briefs, the waistband shot from much use, the material some off-color I was too dispirited to look at very closely. I held the garment away from me for some long seconds, pondering the alternatives. The C.O. looked at me blankly and I had a sudden, clear sense that this was not the time for independent thinking. Rather than stand their naked, I slid the things on feeling, somewhat like the narrator in the famous E.B. White essay, the chill of death at my groin. (In truth, Receiving and Discharge pretty well approximated the basement laundry of a prep-school gymnasium where you jostled with other male bodies in the line to swap out your old jock strap, T-shirt and towel.— Strange how one has been *prepared* in ways one least suspects.)

It wasn't until passing back through Oklahoma City years later that I could appreciate the almost-genteel pleasures of the place.

There was nothing to do here—nothing to be done. Hardly anyone spoke to anyone else. It was quiet; the TV room was separate. The C.O.'s never came out from behind their desk; never hassled anyone. Nothing was expected of you. If you wanted to get some thinking done, this was the place, before you got sucked into the life of some other jail. The major problem was lack of smokes … and the only access to outside was a small courtyard that remained in shadow except for a couple hours when the low spring sun peeked over the western wall.

Sometimes a guy would give you shorts on his cigarette after he was done. Or he'd drop it on the ground so you could pick it up after he walked away, presumably.

Part Two

G.D.s

My first day in Chicago I sat down at a table for lunch and was immediately surrounded by a group of Black men, Gangster Disciples, arms folded across their chests, bemused looks. And a flood of jailhouse clichés came into my head.

"Oh, is this your table?" I asked sweetly.

"Go ahead and finish your lunch," Shorty G said, which I did in a little under a minute.

"Who the fuck are you, some kind of movie star?" he asked later.

"I'm nobody," I said, feeling the full meaning of my words.

I'd arrived at Chicago Metropolitan Correction Center, a 26-story federal jail in Chicago's South Loop, the previous evening. They'd processed me through Receiving & Discharge and brought me up to the unit after lockdown. A Corrections Officer showed me to a cell and locked the door behind me, leaving me to my personal thoughts. Enough ambient light from the hall shone through a narrow window in the door so I could see the guy in the lower bunk curled in fetal position, facing the wall.

I spread a sheet on the top bunk, put an army blanket over that, and stepping lightly on the corner of a wooden desk, flopped onto my back like a high jumper and fell into a hard sleep. I slept through breakfast, got up for lunch and bumbled up to the GD's table without observing things first.

After my little interview with Shorty G, I ate my hamburger in three bites and went back to my section and watched TV the rest of the afternoon. At 4 o'clock they locked us in our cells for count. When the C.O. came by you were supposed to be standing. If you weren't they could give you a "shot," a demerit point of some sort, I guessed.

After count was cleared the C.O. went from door to door with a master key. I walked onto the main floor, got into chow line and stepped expectantly forward. (They'd brought up carts from the kitchen and stowed them in a little utility room.) An inmate handed a couple trays over a Dutch door. Greens and potatoes and chicken. Cake and milk. *Not bad.* And as I turned and looked across the room, inmates sitting shoulder to shoulder, it suddenly felt as if I hadn't a friend in the world.

"Psst, over here," someone called. At a long cafeteria table were a lot of white boys from downstate Illinois who liked to rob banks. Eccentric facial hair, mullets and crooked teeth. The salt of the earth. If you ever wanted a good dose of gallows humor, these were the guys.

"You stay away from Shorty's table now," said this affable hillbilly, all Adam's apple and teeth. Evil was the soul of the party, a sweet guy with a soupçon of the devil, to be sure. My first week I went into his cell and he was wrestling with one of his buddies;

Evil fancied himself some kind of MMA genius; actually, he wasn't wrestling so much as passing out in the grip of a technically sound headlock.

His friend let go and Evil came round shortly. "I need to protect against that shit," Evil said. "Like do a roundhouse to your face."

"Yeah, *right*," said the other fellow, a short, dirty-looking person.

"I'll kick your ass like the cops did," Evil said.

"I'll put your ass to sleep again."

"I'll fuck you up, seriously dude."

"Like the cops fucked *you* up when they found you drinking in that bar!"

"Oh, shit. Like they found *you* running down the street," Evil said, jumping off the bed to tell his favorite story: "This fuckin' jerk tries to rob the bank at two minutes after five. They have the vault locked for the day. He jumps over the counter anyway. There ain't no money there, so he jumps back over the counter and runs out the front door. The bank hits the alarm and the cop cars come and see this guy running down the street."

"They got you just the same, fucker."

"Yeah, but I *got* mine!" Evil, it seems had at least made it as far as the inevitable barroom and proceeded to spend his bounty before the shadow of the law passed over his brow.

That night I lay in the dark smoking menthol cigarettes from shorts my cellie fished out of our ashtray and re-rolled in toilet paper wrapper. His conversation lighted on who was a *Rat*, a *Snitch*....

That stuff didn't interest me at all. I never had a doubt where my loyalties lay. Not with Alhaji or Claire. Not with an organization.

I woke early the next morning and stood on the rail watching guys buff the floors in big, hypnotic sweeping motions. Evil made triple-strength instant coffee. A Jewish-Cherokee named Ron had smokes. We talked crazy. Talked all morning. I was in alcohol withdrawal.

What bothered me was the indignity of renouncing my actions. The way they flung your honor back in your face, as carelessly as flinging a glove. There really was nowhere to set down now, no lunch table, no rhetorical ground.

A Very Short
Game of Scrabble

One morning Evil came over with the Scrabble board. I was sitting on the main floor drinking coffee.

"So, you ready to get your ass beat?" he said,

"Sure," I said.

"You got words?" he said.

Words, words, words. I went through books at a prodigious rate. Four, five a week. The words just went right through without any particular sensibility to oppose them.

One night, with no real idea how, I even tried meditating in order, I guess, to find a new *inner* organization. To stem the loss of words.

How long did this go on? A month or more? This story spans years, though it seems to have happened in days and weeks. It is the foreshortening effect of memory. *(And so, at length, be brief.)*

The game started slowly, monosyllables mostly. Then Evil played *gnarl*.

"What's that?" I said.

"Gnarl."

"Like *Gnarly, dude*?"

"No, *gnarl*. Like *Look at that dog* gnarl *on that bone*."

"Alright, good one," I said. Then I played *leant* off of gnarl.

"What's that?"

"Leant."

"Alright. Good one." Then he played *troth*.

"Like **Horse** *troth*?"

"No, like *loyalty*, dummy."

Court Call

Early one morning the C.O. unlocked my door. "Fillmore," he said, "court call."

Two or three others were up and showering, so I followed suit. In fifteen minutes we were in the elevator on our way to a holding cell in R&D where a bunch of other inmates were sitting around on steel benches.

There was quiet talk. Some guys seemed to know each other. They knew about the various trials going on. They knew some of the guards. Knew stuff in general.

Oh hell, they knew the truth of the matter, which is that they were headed up the river, and they endeavored to go like men.

Even the poor soul from 13 methodically tucking his pant legs inside his socks, taking them back out and tucking them in again, elaborate pleats ironed into his jump suit, woman's nails, hair out to here, was possessed of a quiet dignity.

Eventually they brought in some trays with cold oatmeal and an apple, and we sat around on cold steel benches pensively chewing our breakfast. Afterwards a Mexican inmate dropped his trousers and shat in the metal toilet right there in front of everyone. Happily, some guy pulled a cigarette and matches out of his sock and lit up.

The rattling of chains filled the hallway as the marshals arrived, and in short order they had us moving along a little assembly line. One Marshall patted you down, another put cuffs and a black box on your wrists, while another passed a chain around your waist and secured it to the cuffs. Another put on the leg irons.— And though the Marshalls were definitely the Marshalls and the inmates the inmates, there was a shared if unhappy sense of purpose. Cuffing up was a big drag for everyone involved, so everyone worked in a spirit of cooperation.

"That too tight?"

"Naw, that's okay."

"Okay, move along."

They marched us down a hallway into the sally port and onto a two-ton truck, the Grey Goose, and shut the doors. The sally port was a big concrete garage. Up in the corner behind a small plexi-glass window was "control," the central nervous system of the prison. Instructions from any one of several dozen guards or staff were radioed to control, who fired doors open. You'd here an electric hum, then a clack as the dead bolt shot back, then a buzzer when someone pulled the door open.

Once they had us locked in the truck the Marshalls retrieved their firearms from a steel lockbox inside the front door. (There was a rumor someone escaped once by taking a Marshall's gun out of his holster and shooting the place up—which seemed a very remote possibility; everybody just hobbled complacently along today.) Then the Marshalls climbed in the front of the truck, separated from us by steel mesh, one driving, one standing half in the well, locked and cocked, and a steel door rolled up and the truck sped up a ramp and careened onto the street, followed by a chase car as Marshalls blocked traffic, we inmates, despite ourselves, looking excitedly around as we raced the three or four blocks to Daley Plaza.

In a matter of minutes the truck was safely in the Dirksen Federal Building sally port and we were unloaded and brought up cargo elevators to bullpens outside the courtroom where we sat around waiting for them to uncuff us.

At nine O'clock the Marshalls came and got some guy and led him into the courtroom. Later that morning an old jailer came shuffling along the corridor and called my name out.

"Court," he said, and cuffed my hands in front of me and unlocked the cage and led me in the opposite direction from the courtroom. As we turned a corner he leaned into me and murmured his habitual joke, "I got good news and bad news," he said. "They indicted your lawyer."

Agents Brett and Wayne met me at the end of the hallway and took me down an elevator to the United States Attorney's offices where they removed the cuffs and left me alone with my attorney in a conference room while they went out to get the prosecutor.

I'd interviewed Sean Boland, my attorney, in the legal visiting room at MCC and hired him from a short list of names on the strength of a little press file he'd shown me. He'd gotten some good plea bargains on some big cases, and he seemed to understand my predicament: already having played my hand, to some extent, and trying, still, to leverage a deal.

"Look," he said, "when the prosecutor comes in, we're all on the same side now. If you do this, you have to do it all the way. There's no holding back."

I considered this. "The same side." As if it were so easy. Taken separately, my crime and my impending cooperation posed twin sorrows....

The Assistant US Attorney, an ambitious looking thirty-two-year-old with spectacles, came in the room and introduced himself. I stood up and tentatively held out my hand. He shook cordially, sat down across from me and frankly informed me that if I gave my full cooperation, he would move the judge to grant a 5K1 downward departure from the sentencing guidelines.

The superseding indictment charged the Goddamn Professionals and Carl and Perry and me with conspiring to smuggle 10-30 kilograms of heroin. With my "managerial role," the Federal Sentencing Guidelines stipulated a sentencing range of 188-235 months incarceration, 15-20 years. A 5K1 could take a third to a half off that.

I bristled at their calculation of 10-30 kilos—caused myself some little grief in persevering along this line of thinking, willfully figuring and refiguring the sentencing range in solitary, sobered hours, concocting some mitigating circumstance, some arithmetic error that might restore time.

I agreed, signed a paper saying so, and began a rambling, free form narrative, telling them everything I could think of from my first tentative visit to Chicago to visiting Alhaji in Benin. There was so much it had to be broken up over several sessions. Of course owning up's easy when you're brought up Roman Catholic—the most natural thing in the world. We're possessed of an almost pathological need to confess. And the words poured out like pus from a lanced wound—or healing balm, if you prefer.

How to Make Your Bed

Afterwards, my lawyer and the AUSA went across the hall.

"How is it in there?" Agent Wayne said.

"Ok." I said. How could you describe MCC, anyway? It was altogether worse than one imagined, yet tolerable, almost pleasant at times.

"How's Claire?" I said

Agent Wayne blushed, trying not to look caught off guard. Agent Brett grinned.

"She's … a little freaked out," Agent Wayne said, making toward me to cuff me for the ride back upstairs.

"About her sister's safety, mostly," Agent Brett said.

Seemed like typical Claire. She'd make the most noise. (Of course you told the prosecutor things, careful to play up the danger you were putting yourself in by cooperating. This made your assistance more valuable ... at the same time that it aggravated Alhaji's charges. I wasn't trying to bury anyone.) The thought of Alhaji actually harming any of us seemed almost incredible. He'd made references: "We only use the people from Miami," he would say. Or refer to "hooking" people out of jail, or "putting blood on the floor." But all that referred to other people. Such things may have occurred in Africa and on the South Side, but they didn't happen to us in our story.

"Where've they got her?" I asked.

"Halfway house in San Francisco," they said, crowding about me in their familiar way.

I chewed over this bit of information. *Claire was out on bail.* And for the next five years she'd make her motions asking the judge for home confinement, permission to travel, expungement of home confinement. Work little jobs, make tentative relationships. The thing was, she was still doing time. Except it didn't count.

"You think they'd give me bond now?" I said.

"When you've finished your proffer, maybe."

I thought about it briefly and put it out of my mind. The logic of my actions had led me here. I needed follow that trail wherever it led, for what lay at the end was an image of myself, and in that image some essential truth I'd managed to dodge my whole life.

Back in my cell I tried to make myself at home; mopped the floor, arranged some books on the shelf under the wooden desk and fixed up my bed, stuffing newspapers and magazines between the bedsprings and rubbing baby powder into the mattress. I'd snagged a couple extra sets of sheets and rearranged everything just so and was intent on starting a long letter to L, when the unit door fired and a bunch of people came on the unit and the C.O. yelled, "Shake down. Everyone on the main floor. Now," and sundry Bureau of Prisons personnel with latex gloves, wind breakers and trash bags inundated the unit as the cops herded us onto the main floor, frisking us as we went. I'd tried to get back to my cell to grab a book, but the Captain stopped me. "You, there. Up on the main floor."

So for the next two hours we sat murmuring and craning our necks as the cops threw out our things. You'd see a bunch of stuff come flying out of a cell, a second interval as the guy totted up the damage, followed by a groan of recognition. Of course everything was technically property of the Bureau of Prisons.

Eventually they randomly grabbed half of my books and sent them home despite my protests that I'd had them sent from the publisher, per B.O.P. policy.

So long, Shakespeare.

Otherwise you hoped to find a Signet Classic or two on the woeful little carts they rolled through the unit, in order to lose yourself on some heath in wind and rain at midnight—to lay your mind against a shape, a curve of thought or sensibility, and to be ennobled, yes. Often as not you took a flyer on Chuck Colton's autobiography, Jackie Collins, really bad stuff.

Out of the doors flew extra blankets, steel-toed shoes, porn, jerry-rigged battery packs, work gloves, books, utensils and unidentified miscellany. A Corrections Officer stood there looking perplexedly at a water-filled weight bag we'd made in the corner room out of trash bags and a mesh laundry bag. It's surprising how much stuff you can accumulate, all of it and none of it necessary.

When they called our section out, the Associate Warden was standing by my door.

"Bag all this stuff up," he said.

I looked down at the wreckage of my bed. "Cock*sucker,*" I said—not my usual verbiage, but it expressed my frustration.

"You call me?" the A.W. said.

"Wha?" I said.

" Nobody … call … me … any … other … thing!" he said. No!" I said.

"Tell you what," the A.W. said, regaining his composure. "Grab your i.d. and meet me up on the main floor, son." And taking up his walkie-talkie he said, "One-one hotel. I've got one for the hole."

This was bad. You didn't want to go to the hole. You didn't want to mess up your security status, for one thing. And you didn't want to wind up getting sent to another floor upon return from the hole, where no one knew you; it was easy to forget how much time it took to build up goodwill. I remember some time later taking the elevator back from rec and stopping at the law library where some Vice Lords from another floor got on; I was joking with Main—an enforcer with the Vice Lords, a tough kid who had the habit of throwing his head back and looking down his nose at you, a gesture he must have found useful in unmanning men twice his age—I was joking with Main about a layup he'd missed when this guy, his co-defendant, this crooked cop, T-Fly, took exception. "You shut your motherfucking mouth," T-Fly said, taking a half step toward me. And I looked at Main and he looked back at me, sad-like, and there was nothing I could do about it; I just stood there looking down at my feet.

Certainly being stripped of all your belongings and sent into a dirty, empty cell with another troublemaker was discouragement enough. But it wasn't even the material stuff, from whose claims one was at pains to disentangle oneself—for to become attached to material comfort is weak. It was that I'd had enough.

You could smell the beast languishing down there on the eleventh floor: tales of fellows naked with excrement smeared in their hair; pride and foolishness crushed by a terrible kind of peristalsis. That was real life down there. For those poor souls like me who had not quite come to terms with life, who had not under-stood that life is earnest and hard and had needed to stick their hands into the hornet's nest to feel alive, being sent to prison was enough. I had had enough. I had no illusions about resisting.

As long as one remained in compliance, one had a semblance of rights. Step off that path and you fell into an abyss. One was grateful to learn that lesson, for there are those on whom it is wasted, those thrill-seekers—you meet them in the world—who can't seem to get close enough to the heat or the action or the knife's edge until it is too late, and even then I suspect there are those in heaven or hell who would brag their death was more radical than the next guy's. There is an urge to court disaster. An "imp of the perverse," it's true.

I was standing by the elevator looking at my i.d. Three-eight-seven-four-nine-O-five-four. The O-five-four signified Southern District of New York. I didn't know about the rest. Technically we were still on lockdown, but John Allen came up to me on the main floor.

"What are you doing, Fillmore?"

John was a good guy. He was active in the Muslim community, always ready with an *As-Salaam-Alaikum*. I'd enjoyed talking with him about spiritual matters.

"I'm going to the hole."

"What'd you do?"

"A.W. thinks I called him a cocksucker."

He laughed. "Go apologize."

"Really?"

"Go apologize."

In fact I did feel bad. I liked the A.W. Whereas the Captain and the Lieutenant had a gangsterish air about them—were ticked off that they had become babysitters, essentially—and the Warden merely absented himself, the A.W. used to come right down on the floor shaking hands. Ok, that was weird, I guess, and an affront to some who felt his behavior *Tommish*. But I liked him for the very reason so many guys didn't.

"Excuse me, sir. Can I talk with you for a minute?" I said when he came up onto the floor.

"What is it?"

I apologized.

"Well, it looks like it's your lucky day, son; we've got a full house down on eleven. Get back to your cell."

I don't know how things might have turned out otherwise. In my experience, calamity comes on wings of silk. Disaster rarely looks disastrous. It might seem all the same to you; what's the difference between one floor and another? I don't know. I had a distinct impression I had made a narrow escape. John, wherever you are, Thank you and *Wa-Alaikum-Salaam.*

Native Sons

Over the next few weeks I felt myself slipping into the life of the prison; turned deliberately away from the view of Van Buren Street fifteen floors below—pedestrians crossing beneath the el, the curving track, a flight of pigeons—and surveyed my surroundings: an equilateral triangle all concrete block and linoleum; double tiers on the back wall, wrought iron rail, showers top and bottom and televisions in the two angles with a cluster of rubber chairs; a little kitchen and microwave with a view of the South side on the second wall; a day room with a ping pong table and book cart on the third; the C.O.'s desk sitting atop the apex. Above the unit door there was a clock on the wall, a closet with cleaning supplies and a metal locker with game boards. Within this box—and isn't the most fantastic view of sea and sky still a box?—life went on in its various, colorful forms.

I had a strange, brief conversation with a guy in the shower one evening. He was in a gang on the West Side, a million dollar operation, charged in one of those sweeping conspiracies, one of the Masterson clan, a Vice Lord. The younger, educated, doted-upon brother, he was berating himself for having known better.

"There are two kinds of guys up in here," he said suddenly: "those who are telling and those who wish they were."

The latter kind of guy, he waited for his sentence to come down, beyond hope of reprieve or succor, while his brother, Bay-Bay, rallied, cajoled, berated the troops like on the street.

A couple days later he transferred to another floor, hateful no doubt to listen to Bay-Bay all day long, robbed even of his own thoughts....

How did you take men who were (so) absolute? Who every day sacrificed themselves for lost causes? How did you take men who created their own rules at the same time they assented to a fate that had been arranged for them? And how did you square that with your own choices?

I knew them for a time, then fell away, energies spent, as they streamed brilliantly out of this world. Some will gain their freedom as old men. Others are serving life sentences in Florence, Colorado and Marion, Illinois, in solitary 6x8 cells.

(The Bureau of Prisons makes no secret that it uses Supermax prisons to gag gang leaders like legendary Gangster Disciple leader Larry Hoover, who allegedly orchestrated numerous, increasingly political activities from a state prison cell. But such men are not a threat because they possess dangerous minds; they incite dangerous thoughts in ordinary minds.)

You didn't just go near Shorty G. or address him actually, unless it was on the basketball court, where normal social conventions relaxed. I recall him skipping backward on defense after hitting a running layup. "I'm no scrub, you know," he said, laughing.

In Disciple boss Hoover's absence, Shorty had commanded 30,000 people in Chicago alone. Though no one accused him of being a visionary like Hoover, he was a good number two man, a loyal soldier who kept the work going. Now he was up against a federal prosecution by FBI and U.S. Attorney cum gubernatorial aspirant Jim Burns dubbed "Operation Headache," aimed at the upper echelon of G.D. "governors."

Shorty had to be accounted for every four hours, so he just sat at his table on the main floor (the very seat I'd mistakenly sat in my first day). Ultimately he was headed for Florence ADX, the new administrative supermax in Colorado, his life slipping away in a kind of horrific slow motion.

He was sitting in front of the television, legs planted on the bottom rung of the TV stand, smoking a Black and Mild.

I'd slept through a prison convocation of some sort. Everyone was down in the gym, all six or seven floors (the men if only to get a look at the women). A motivational speaker had come, which was unprecedented, downright odd in fact, as MCC rarely if ever strayed from its prescribed function of keeping the physical animal fit to stand trial, nothing more; but I'd fallen asleep after dinner and missed the proceedings and found myself alone on the floor with Shorty. It was eerie. We were the only two guys on the unit. I came out of my cell and kind of edged my way over and sat down.

"You're not going to the thing?" I asked. It was a stupid question.

"Naw, I'm not trying to hear any of that stuff." He sat there, neither inviting me in nor pushing me away.

Shorty was another guy that you truly couldn't imagine on the street. Apparently he was a sharp dresser, and he drove a Rolls. In his orange jumpsuit, though, he looked merely short. His head was shaved clean and he had a slight goggle-eyed expression. He was

serious, though, and he had a certain kind of magnetism. He supposedly seduced the head of some gang task force in the Chicago
P.D. Was fucking her all along. Something made you want to get
near him, made you want him to open up to you. The thing was,
there was nothing in it for him.

He described a type that I'd been drawn to my whole life—
after my own father—that was self-sufficient … and emotionally
closed. I picture them, one and all, gazing into the distance as if
crossing some imaginary Delaware.

My infatuation with Alhaji was just another iteration, I was
fairly certain, of a desire to stand next to greatness. What that ever
accomplished, I couldn't say, but I persisted….

There was ultimate fighting on television: two guys in a cage
preparing to rend one another. It was the first time I'd ever seen it,
and I was surprised they were showing it on our normally-chaste
T.V., and shorty's eyes got a little wider as if he, too, couldn't believe
his good luck.

"Oh, I love some violence," he said.

I looked over at him shifting in his seat.

"Punch old Roy right in the gut, watch all the giardiniera
peppers and shit come spillin' out." Roy was a greasy jailhouse
lawyer who helped Shorty with his legal work, as much for his own
aggrandizement as for Shorty's sake, and it seemed to pain Shorty
to have to countenance Roy's fawning.

Roy always had a bowl of some jailhouse garbage—ramen
noodles with Dorito chips crumbled on top, and a healthy garnish
of giardiniera peppers. He'd be walking around chewing and
talking.

"Stomp all on his ankles; stomp that shit. Giardiniera peppers
all on the floor and shit," he growled.

Shorty was fair, though. Later, when I bunked with Frank Collins,
a stock broker, I heard Shorty ream out his guys one day. "You let

Mr. Collins watch what he wants. He don't bother anyone. I don't care. You let him watch *Andy Griffith* if he wants." And old Frank blushed like a girl.

The fighters squared off. A punch or two was thrown. Then one fighter shot for the other's legs and they both went down to the canvas. The fighter on top scurried to side mount the fellow on the bottom, who'd gotten a grip on the other's wrist and was patiently trying to bend it inwards.

I glanced at Shorty out of the corner of my eye. He took his ease, while the fight had me all out of sorts.

"I remember my first dime," Shorty said, gazing wistfully into his past. "In the motherfuckin' D.O.C. Not this shit...."

Shorty had served time for murder, had worked himself up the corporate ladder of Discipledom somehow, and found himself now at a crossroads with the law. A rise and fall. A life completed in about 37 years.

The fighter on top grabbed the other guy's wrist to prevent him from getting too much torque, and they turned like that in a clockwise direction, a quarter turn at a time, the fighter on the bottom attempting to step outside his opponent's legs and drive him on his back as the other danced out of the way.

There were questions I wanted to ask Shorty, but you didn't just ask questions in jail. So we sat and watched the fight, enjoying the simple, clean act of physical aggression.

How strange to think of him now, so many years later, in a tiny cell underground—sitting on the edge of a poured concrete bed, elbows on knees, staring past the steeple of his fingers.

No book tells his story. A few Trib articles from 1996. Marginalia in some GD fan page.... Here was a man, once, reduced to a mere proposition about ... what? The prerogative of the state? The expendability of human life? You tell me.

Strange Cellies

There's a domesticity that develops between cellies. Even fellows you might consider odious desire to spend their time with a sympathetic soul. It's funny to see them toddling off to their cells for lockdown, old married couples: the Crack-Dealers, the Carjackers.

So when your cellie leaves, you do your best to find someone who doesn't seem likely to shank you in the middle of the night, and you put in a request. Otherwise, if you get greedy, hoping to keep a single for any length of time, you're liable to get the next fellow walking through the door. And it ain't gonna be Fred Astaire. I've made this mistake a few times.

You wake up in the middle of the night, for instance, choking on cigarette smoke; your new cellie has blocked the air vents for some reason he is not quite prepared to explain and is applying a faux wood-grain to cardboard picture frames with a nauseous concoction of cigarette butts and coffee, and he's chain smoking and singing along in full voice to his headphones.

Another one (no English) is running the hot water with the vents blocked to create a sauna-like atmosphere (*again*—what is it with the vents?) and he's practicing some kind of esoteric martial art, making crazy, frightening gesticulations with his hands, and he's spraying undiluted cleaner around the room and, *yes, that's the unit toilet scrubber—the one that 88 guys scrub 44 shit-stained toilets with—in your sink.*

Yet another has got some kind of funk emanating from his locker. You try your best to ignore it until one day you're seized by a fit of anaphylactic sneezing, and only after you threaten him with physical violence does he finally gets off his ass and rummage through the pile of shit thrown in there to discover a ruptured carton of milk fizzing away.

A lot of guys have racial preferences. Basically, I'm looking for a cellie who, as I say, seems (1) unlikely to visit gratuitous violence on me in the middle of the night; any semblance of (2) sanity and (3) hygiene is totally serendipitous.

But it never occurred to me that *I* might be the strange cellie....

As far as I was concerned, I was just going through an introspective phase. My case was in one of those inactive periods where you hear nothing from your lawyer for months on end. There aren't even status hearings. (In fact the US Attorney was working on the second superseding indictment in my case.) And so you get carried away by one preoccupation or another: working out, or reading or something.

I just didn't want to get out of my bunk. With the exception of meals and rec, which I never did miss in four years, I just didn't want to move. And so my little collection of books grew up around me, and I lay there for hours fruitlessly reworking poems and doing crossword puzzles and listening to the radio.

Of course the lovely thing about pretrial is they can't make you work. The result is that men tend to throw themselves into trivial pastimes with all the energy of men who have nothing better to do. And I threw myself into my lethargy with a singleness of purpose.

My cellmate seemed to come and go without a care. And my stack of books grew up around me.

Not that he was up to anything so important, it seemed to me, unless you consider interminable hands of Hearts or Casino or whatever he played "important." But I'm getting ahead of myself. I had no idea anything was wrong and felt not a whit of animus.

You know how it is, then, when suddenly you discover the little mosquito of annoyance has been whining away at the edge of your consciousness. All of a sudden I realized something was wrong. Then Evil came up to me.

"Hey, man. You gotta let your cellie have the room once in awhile. And, uh, take a shower. You stink."

"Really?"

"Yup."

So I showered. But apparently the damage was done. Now that things were up front, my cellie wanted me out. Funny, I can't remember him actually saying so, just that I felt it coming, the way you know you're going to get sacked at work.

"You want me out?" I said it for him.

"Yup."

Now I was going to have to find someone with an open bed and go ask him if I could, you know, move in.

Fuck.

I considered my options.

There were GDs, Vice Lords, Latin Kings, Outlaw Bikers, a Whitman's Sampler of drug dealers from Gary, Indiana, and old Frank Collins, a stock broker.

"Hey, Frank. Do you think I could move in here?

"Suit yourself," he said, graciously.

We bunked together for about a year, started up a scrabble foursome, fifty cents a game, really terrific play. That's until Frank figured Ron Baumgarter, the Jewish Cherokee, was surreptitiously discarding the Q. Either he'd play piqued or qat (a non-U favorite) or some such word, or you'd reach into the bag on your last turn, the U's all played, and pull out the Q. And so the game broke up.

Then things just sort of went south between Frank and me. I got impatient with him. Things that had seemed endearing annoyed me. What had seemed like character now seemed boorish. He was an unseemly and venal old man. I caught him listening for the guy who filled the candy machines. As soon as the unit door fired, Frank would be out the door like a cat, pockets filled with quarters so he could corner the market on peanut butter cups. One holiday weekend he even had the audacity to charge me double for cigarettes. "Forget it, Frank. I quit," I said. (And I did.)

I started hanging with some other guys. Words were exchanged; I don't remember why. It's possible that with the proximity of people in jail, relationships live and die at an accelerated rate, accomplishing what usually takes five or ten or twenty years in a matter of months. Those days it seemed like everyone was walking around saying, "yeah, he used to be a good dude, I don't know what the fuck happened." I only remember feeling ashamed for telling Frank he'd look damn silly with his head stuck in the toilet. Whether he had it coming or not, it's just not a nice thing to say to a sixty-year-old man.

I moved out to room with another guy a few cells down. All the tension of the previous weeks disappeared. I got down to a new routine. Life began to interest me all over again. Though sometimes I'd see Frank at dinner with his new cellie, chatting and laughing, and I'd feel a little pang almost like jealousy.

Jimmy Dharma

One morning there were two new guys on the upper tier sitting in lotus position. Jimmy Dharma had come straight from Dharmsala, India where he'd been living up in the hills amid tall trees and baboons, the Tibetan government in exile encamped below ... and Ricky from who-knows-where, Illinois, spun on acid, grinning un-accountably. I introduced myself after breakfast. Jimmy and Ricky were looking at a book by a Tibetan Lama.

"Hey I noticed you guys up on the tier," I said.

"Yeah?" Jimmy said.

"Can I, you know, hang with you guys?" I said, getting straight to the point. There was no sense in being coy. It was like they'd fallen from a clear blue sky. There wasn't exactly a surplus of buddhists in MCC Chicago.— Sure, you could find yourself a bible study, or head down to the law library for *Jumah* (where in addition to whatever spiritual nourishment you took it was still possible to murmur with co-defendants from other floors about pretrial motions for an hour or so.) I just wasn't interested in submitting myself to a doctrine. I was still invested in my own mind. And while many of the faithful must have felt that they were reserving a part of themselves from the prison, I saw it as just another form of surrender. In Buddhism I suspected something else....

Each morning we met on the main floor at six, ate breakfast, then retired to a little mezzanine near the counselor's office to do our yoga, meditate and study dharma with the zeal of monks.

It was really honest and spare and beautiful. And in the insular world of jail, where it's all too easy to "rock the boat," as Jimmy used to say, it's also possible to spread peace.

Sooner or later, whatever white inmates were on the floor would come sniffing around, if only to express cynicism. One day John came by.

"Oh-oh, here comes trouble," Jimmy said laughing. He had an endearing habit of indulging his own cynical nature, but would immediately check himself. "He looks like a "little lost puppy," he said to Ricky and me. "Come here puppy...."

John had a bad case of resentment about everyone and everything. They'd discovered his embezzlement scheme almost immediately, and he found himself in jail before the first flush of his success had worn off. He was still fuming.

What were they arguing about? John was shooting his mouth off: "The only thing I trust is my M16," he said.

Jimmy wasn't having it. Tall and tattooed with arcane tantric symbols on his chest, he exuded 70s L.A. hip. A street kid who'd graduated into something of a hoodlum, he'd been in the system before, a bunch of places, but Terminal Island was where he had matriculated, for one seems to have been schooled in the finer points of jailhouse deportment at one institution or another. In short, he knew his way around.

But more than that he was possessed of an unshakeable conviction. I think that Jimmy, having landed himself back in prison on a probation violation (he'd left the U.S. illegally then come walking right back into the country, and jail, to save his son from gang-life), was in the midst of an epiphany and was speaking with an authority you only get when you've got nothing else and the truth is speaking right through you.

"What are you talking about, Lame?"

"I mean I trust my gun."

"Don't give me that stuff."

"What stuff?

"That Marine stuff."

"I *am* a Marine."

"You're not a Marine, you're in jail."

"So."

"So, what about *John*? What does *John* want?"

"What do *I* want?"

"Yeah. What do *you* want?"

"I don't want anything. I want to get the fuck out of here."

"No you don't."

"I don't, hah?"

"No. You know what you want?"

"What, what do I want?"

"You want a hug."

"Huh?"

"You want a hug."

"The fuck are you talking about?"

"You want a hug? I'll give you one."

"Fuck you."

"Come on, you want a hug, I'll give you a hug…."

It's funny to hear this dialog as I write it; it doesn't sound quite right. Anyone in his right head would have laughed it off. But I think John was feeling so vulnerable and so fooled with, and so *untenable*, that as he started to yell back at Jimmy something caught in his throat and he went shrill.

And a change came over him. That supercilious demeanor of the social conservative—the frat boy—so hardened, just split open and fell away like a husk. Then the usual things: working out, doing origami, whatever, John threw himself into them with an intensity. You got through a game of chess with him utterly ground down. Not that he ever came up to the second floor and did the Dog Pose with us—he kept a distance from all that, a physical and ironical distance; but it was an informed irony, as if he'd been reading about things, thinking about things.

(I want to imagine him now, after all these years, rising early one morning and standing in the middle of his cell, utterly quiet, despairing, and no other gesture possible, bringing his hands together over his head and going onto his knees and prostrating himself full length on the floor … feeling the morning cold of the linoleum, the hum of the building's machinery deep in his chest, the sorrow, the ecstasy, the terror, the endlessness, all of it.)

Monday morning. Dead Man's Pose. Salutation to the Sun. Jimmy and Ricky and I snagged a corner of the top tier by the Counselor's office. Most other inmates had gone back to bed after breakfast; a few looked on, dubious.

In the Heart Sutra, Avalokiteshvara Buddha talks about emptiness, circling all the way back to the four noble truths, starting place of Buddhism: "Also, there is no Truth of Suffering / Of the Cause of Suffering, / Of the Cessation of Suffering, Nor the Path // There is no Wisdom, and there is no Attainment whatsoever / because there is nothing to be attained."

It was a triumphant punk rock rejection of all of its own glorious bullshit. A self-deconstruction. Like peeling back bandages to find underneath the scars a palpable human flesh after all.

Later that night I got into a basketball game in basement rec, spoke up for myself when they asked who had next. Not yet schooled in the rules of the dance, I merely ran up and down the court, set an accidental screen for Boo-G Strawman who stepped around his man and with a little flip dished me the ball under the hoop so unexpected and so slick that I actually ducked thinking there must be someone *else behind* me—the ball hitting the crash pad with a little thud and hanging there an instant before dropping, a dead weight, to the floor, Shorty, Boo-G, Head Carson, et. al. actually astonished at this brilliant refutation of the conventional self … before erupting into laughter.—

(Some time shortly after, all those GD governors went for their sentencing. The last I saw of them they stood in the hallway waiting for the elevator, Shorty and the others, shifting their weight, nervous as grooms on their wedding day.

(After the guilty verdict was read they whisked them from court straight to the penitentiary in Terre Haute.

Tuesday morning. Dog pose. Running in place. Shaking out our hands. And I am laughing and laughing; it is like something has opened up and a great gust of wind is blowing straight up my anus and out the top of my head.

I Am Handcuffed to the Chair

My testimony culminated in the grand jury room, where I read a statement prepared by Assistant United States Attorney Mary MacBride, who had taken over the case. You got the impression she had a heart and a moral sense along with the mandate to prosecute criminals. She was the sort of person you overlooked, with her pageboy haircut and prim suit, then read about years later in the alumni newsletter.)

Twelve citizens of Chicago sat in a small room in a jury box looking blandly back at me: someone's grandmother, a housewife, the jury foreman with his sleeves rolled up, business-like. I was about to sit down when Agent Brett took me gently by the elbow, murmured "Sorry" and handcuffed me to the chair.

After recovering my dignity to some extent, I told my story. I'd repeated it so many times, it seemed utterly inane to me now, and I tried to enliven my recitation for the jury—lent emphasis in odd places, stressed the unexpected word. It was a strange performance. "Interesting delivery," AUSA MacBride said afterwards.

A month or so later there was a status hearing. The courtroom was crowded. Kyle was in front of Judge Norgle entering a plea of 'not guilty' as a Marshall led me into the dock at the side of the room. There was a stirring. Hester, the Kids, the Goddamned Professionals, Temper and Zane … were present, looking, from a distance, well, like they had fists jammed up their asses. Everyone, minor and major participants alike, had been named in the superseding indictment—even those like Temper who'd never actually carried, but despite their pretend outrage had materially advanced the conspiracy in one way or another.

Judge Norgle granted each defendant bond and they all fled back home. Apparently I wasn't going to have any company in the bullpen that day, but my presence in the courtroom was no accident. In my orange jumpsuit I was a palpable warning to the others.

After a few months and some brief posturing by attorneys, everyone changed his plea to guilty and subsequently met with prosecutors to tell his or her story.

Alhaji remained a fugitive for the moment, whether still running heroin or laying low I couldn't say.

They had his phone numbers. I'd supposed that's how the agents identified him—this person they claimed to be Alhaji—to begin with.

Unable to fast-track extradition, they'd talked of making a prison of Nigeria, but I suspected they wanted more. Alhaji had applied for a visa at the German consulate using an alias. They had him on their radar. Did he know that they were watching?

Time dragged on. I crossed off the days and months from a calendar taped on the wall next to my bunk. Cellies came and went. (I acquired an impressive collection of pornography.)

Finally they called me down to the visiting room one morning. Agents Brett and Wayne were waiting with a government attorney in a windowless legal room. The attorney opened a briefcase and pulled out a photo spread of a half dozen Black men.

"We need you to identify Alhaji," they said.

They'd caught Alhaji, or someone they believed to be Alhaji, at Heathrow Airport in England, incredibly. A routine stop revealed he was carrying undeclared cash and a follow-up investigation turned up an Interpol warrant. Now he was being held at Brixton Prison.

At the time I had an imperfect understanding of this. They didn't quite come out and tell you everything. (Agents are chronically stingy with details.) But I managed to piece together a rough outline with a little help from my attorney.

There was a table and a chair and the two lawyers and the two agents bumping into one another in the small room.

I suppressed a laugh as they handed over the photos. The horizontal scale was all off. It looked like something you got in a photo booth at an arcade. You could imagine each of the fellows in the line-up eating cotton candy and making cross-eyes at the camera, sticking out a powder-blue tongue.

In truth I was terrified that I couldn't identify Alhaji. My mind raced over each detail of each face, coaxing, extrapolating, erasing, overlaying, yet nothing matched the search image in my brain, and so I laughed as one laughs at an earnestly proffered absurdity, a roasted porcupine set steaming in front of you.

"Ok, not number one," I said. "And definitely not number five. Maybe number two, or number four. No, not number four."

"Take your time," Agent Wayne said, pacing back and forth. The others looked politely away as if we were standing at a row of urinals.

"Not number one or four or five. Wait…."

Whether it was the years that had intervened, or that Alhaji had put on weight, I absolutely couldn't pick him out. I pictured him as I remembered him. When Alhaji looked at you sometimes you saw the whites of his eyes beneath the pupil, as if he were bored, or nodding.

I remembered him in different attitudes: enraged at a store clerk who'd given him cheek; unrestrained joy the time I brought him a Nike track suit; but mostly it was the coolness of one who's figured out the angles. *Shakara*, the Nigerians call it, or bluff.

Of course like any politician he never let on. Instead he asked you if you believed in God….

In the photos, the men's eyes were dark. The various facial hair schemes were no clue either. I simply couldn't recognize Alhaji's face. And I realized that I was not going to be able to recognize it. Though I could conjure his voice at will—the resounding tenor punctuated by suppressed digestive misfires—it was as if his face had disappeared.

I finally settled on a photo and the agents dismissed me, looking disgruntled.

Back in jail I worked out vigorously on the dip bar, washed my sweatshirt in a waste bin and hung it by the radiator, re-iced some leftovers in my sink and lay back in my bunk and started a long letter to L. She was in Honolulu now, living by herself. My lonely sweetie. I imagined her on Kalakaua Avenue in Waikiki, by the statue of Duke Kahanamoku, sunlight in her eyes, laughing….

Snake Carver

A couple of days later it came out on the news that this guy on the unit was charged with soliciting young boys on the internet. When he came back from court, a dozen guys were yelling insults from the rail.

Snake Carver, resident O.G. at the moment, called for calm. "Let that man have his day in court," he yelled above the din. Carver was a thirty-five year old con from L.A. who wore a moustache and intimidated people with his psycho routine, working out long hours and generally taking the hardline convict position on any kind of jailhouse question. (He was intrigued by me, though; it tickled him to see a white boy in jail.)

That afternoon I went down to the guy's cell—the sex offender—to see if he was all right. I liked him, liked listening to his crazy conspiracy theories the way one liked reading tabloids at the grocery. He looked like a big baby, hairless and ruddy-cheeked. He seemed utterly harmless.

Carver was just leaving the section with one of his minions as I came down the stairs, and we passed each other wordlessly.

The guy was sitting on his bunk, holding himself, tears in his eyes.

"You've got to check yourself into the hole. Get the hell out of here," I said.

"I didn't do anything. I'm not going to run," he said.

"They don't care."

"But I didn't *do* anything," he said.

I went back to my cell to brood. Jimmy Dharma, said to stay out of it.

Jimmy knew Snake Carver from Terminal Island, where he'd done his first bid, just a street kid in jail for jacking drug dealers, before he became Buddhist. Though he and Carver generally avoided one another, having radically different ideas about life, they had a mutual, grudging respect that verged on affection. I think each man saw in the other some reflection of himself, if only proper jailhouse deportment ... and a moustache ... which is actually a kind of proper jailhouse deportment.

Each had been shaped on a cellular level by prison. To deprive them of its organizing principle would be like stripping away the physical laws of repulsion and attraction that held matter in place. Jimmy found in prison a ground to practice dharma, a nominal existence one might overcome by contemplation of its inherent "emptiness," And he found there, too, a refuge from the vicissitudes of heroin addiction. Carver merely remained obdurate, *more* "himself" all the time. "Keep on doing what you're doing," he said. "That's what they want you to do."

The mood on the floor had turned ugly now. There was an undercurrent rippling the surface. Jimmy said to stay out of it. This was how things got taken care of in prison.

I couldn't stand it, though. I was filled with a righteousness in those days—had in fact given *myself* over to an idea, for there is time and incentive in prison to follow ideas to their logical conclusion, or tentative conclusion, or false conclusion—and for a brief, glorious moment I strode through the unit. For some reason that was not entirely clear to me I wanted to save this kid; wanted to save myself; wanted to save all of us.

Officer Newborn was sitting there blinking. He must have gotten some kind of neurological damage in Desert Storm.

"Are you just going to let this happen?" I said.

He sat there for a moment, then blinked a half dozen times in rapid succession.

"Man, get that fucking guy off the unit," I yelled.

Newborn blinked again, looked at his watch and called for count.

As I was returning to my cell Snake Carver was on the rail screaming at me, really screaming, bits of spittle flying out of his mouth: "People get killed for that shit, they fucking get *killed*."

Generally, you didn't want to talk to the Corrections Officers too much; it could only mean you were snitching on another inmate, which is not how things were done in jail. If you had a problem with someone you took it up behind closed doors—or else you did the genteel thing and dropped a mop ringer off the tier onto their head.

What I didn't know was that they'd gotten to the guy already, had thrown a blanket over his head so he couldn't see and beat the shit out of him. Carver thought I was telling the C.O.

"People get fucking killed," he screamed.

But Newborn was locking Carver's section in, so Carver went back to his cell, greatly agitated, before he could finish his thought.

The next morning they handed our breakfast trays into our cells and locked the doors again, and we remained on lockdown over the next four days as they systematically brought us out to be interviewed.

Eventually they got around to me. In the Counselor's office were two F.B.I. Agents. Of course the routine was familiar.

Did I know what happened to the inmate? they asked.

"Somebody beat him up."

Did I see who did it?

"No."

Was I sure?

"Yes."

And that was it. They never found anything out.

Shortly after, Carver left for the federal medical center in Rochester, Minnesota after having several grand mal seizures. Then he was back.

"I can't figure you," he said one morning as he was working out on the main floor. He exercised at a crisp pace, pushing himself, all the while keeping up a running monologue with his protégés, who hung about the rail.

"Some guys in here will tell you they want to change," he said. "Why would you change who you are? Why would you want to change who you are when you're so close to the truth?"

The cadences of Carver's argument bore into my ear as I sat on the main floor, and I thought of Satan lying chained in hell in *Paradise Lost:* "Hail horrors, hail / Infernal world, and thou profoundest Hell / Receive thy new Possessor: One who brings / A mind not to be changed by place or time. / The mind is its own place, and in itself / Can make a Heaven of Hell, a Hell of Heaven. / What matter where, If I still be the same, / And what I should be."

Carver couldn't figure me because I was a pragmatist—and opportunist. What was there to figure?

Jimmy Dharma was long gone, and though I continued to meditate each morning, something had changed. It wasn't that

Jimmy had reverted to a convict code back in the cell that day when he said to stay out of it—that was his own failing. It was that I was bored. My time was running down and I was trying to stay busy to keep from going crazy.

"You need a workout partner?" I asked Carver.

You see, I didn't care anymore; I was hungry for information. I wanted to get inside this guy's head. I wanted to see how things worked.

Typewriter

So when the typewriter broke, I did the natural thing and brought it up to the Corrections Officer, who stowed it behind his desk.

"You did what?" Carver yelled.

"I put in a work order...."

"You gave our typewriter back to them?"

"So they could fix it."

"They're not going to fix it. They're not going to fix anything. You give them that typewriter and you'll never see it again."

"So maybe they can get us another."

"Yeah, you know, we do our legal work on that typewriter, mother-fucker. What do you want me to do, hand-write my motions?"

I'd tangled with Carver over the typewriter before, when he got wind I was typing out poems. Now I always made sure I had some kind of legal work in case someone came in my cell while I was typing my stuff out. And I always typed out some legal-sounding things at the end in case someone unwound the ribbon to see what had been typed.

"I didn't know. I thought they'd just fix it"

"No, you didn't know. You don't know *shit*."

"I didn't know. This isn't exactly my reality, Carver."

That got him going on one of his favorite rants. "Oh, this is your reality, alright. I guarantee you. You did something to get yourself in here. This is your reality, alright," Carver yelled, working himself up.

"I don't...."

"You don't what? You don't belong in here?" Carver laughed. "Let me tell you something: you belong here. That's your problem is you keep trying to tell yourself you don't belong here."

Carver was right, of course.

"I'm going to get it back," I said. "I'm going to fix it."

"Yeah, you fix it."

I went back up to the C.O.'s desk.

"I made a mistake, Newborn. The typewriter's fine."

Back in my cell, I took everything off my desk and placed the typewriter squarely in the middle and looked it over: a turquoise Olivetti Lettera 32, a slim, heavy machine whose tock-tock-tock could generally be heard, if one listened for it, behind the din of prison. A singular voice of sanity. If its innards were designed as intelligently and as elegantly as the outer-machine, I should have a chance of fixing it, in spite of the fact that I had no mechanical aptitude whatever—had never in my life put together a model airplane or assembled a toy or done anything more than fix the chain on a bicycle.

But I knew the machine. Had accustomed myself to its action. A typewriter like that, you punched at the keys, stabbed at them with your fingers like a Kung Fu master going for a pressure point.

When you typed something out you were certain of it. On a machine like that, language is visceral.

I pushed the carriage back and forth; something had broken so that it free-floated on its bearings. I pulled the top cover off and stared down at the type, arrayed like cards.

Even with no tools or spare parts it might yet be possible to find out what the problem was and try to fix it, the whole afternoon ahead of me.

I lifted the typewriter, an imposing weight, all steel, and shook it. Something rattled inside. I shook again and a little metal tab fell on the desk. I peered down inside, tilting the machine at different angles. Something wasn't right. I tipped the typewriter over and looked through the bottom, moving the carriage back and forth. The drawstring meant to pull the carriage had no tension.

Reaching inside with a plastic knife, I unhooked the drawstring from the carriage. The drawstring wound round a reel. Inside the reel, the mainspring had come unmoored. A tab it attached to had broken off. There was still a little piece left, which I bent over, feeling the metal begin to crumble as I did so, hesitating, contemplating bending the tab back over to check ... a fatal mistake, like all the fatal mistakes of my life, which I avoided now.

I gently hooked the spring back onto the tab, wound the mainspring five or six turns and paid the string back out and hooked it to the carriage. Sat there just looking at it, my finger itching to take it all apart again.

Physics

One afternoon I went up to the C.O.'s desk to talk to Officer Grabowski, an Andy-Kaufmanesque hack who sat there chain smoking Sobranies and reading physics.

Encouraged by my experiments with the typewriter, I suppose, I'd been looking into cosmology and become troubled by the notion of an infinitely expanding universe. The idea seemed abhorrent to me. That everything might collapse back into a singularity every hundred billion years before being reshuffled and dealt back out satisfied some kind of aesthetic urge. But cosmologists seemed to be having a tough time locating sufficient matter to check the escape velocity of everything.

So, I was consulting Grabowski.

"What do you want, Fillmore?" he asked in ironic, high-pitched, Slavic accent.

"Grabowski," I said, "what do you know about, you know, *singularities?*"

This seemed to pique his interest, mostly because I wasn't trying to bum a cigarette.

"Singularities," he said. "You're talking about end of the world."

"Yeah," I said.

Grabowski put down his book, lit a Sobranie and leaned back in his chair.

"What are you up to, Fillmore?" he asked with a smirk.

"I'm not up to anything. I was just thinking about it."

"You were just thinking about it."

"Suppose that everything is just drifting away."

"So?"

"And the universe is falling apart."

"Yeah?"

"And that's it."

"So, what are you asking me?"

"That doesn't bother you somehow?"

"No. Why should it bother me?"

"Everything we are or ever were, the record of life on earth, no: life anywhere, sentience, form, matter, flung out into space? I mean, I don't think I believe in God exactly, but…."

And the mention of God seemed to push some button in him.

"Look, Fillmore. I think this is it. What you see is what you get."

I wasn't prepared for this kind of conversation, with a nihilist, I mean.

"What do you want from me, Fillmore?"

"Nothing, Grabowski."

As I walked back to my cell I heard a muffled sort of commotion. The Masterson boys, Head and Main, had Trinnie Mason trapped under his bunk and were lying on their sides kicking at him with steel-toed shoes. A bunch of guys were laughing at trailer trash waving their fingers in each other's faces on *Jerry Springer*. No. There was an order to the universe. And I felt a lightness in my step.

The Man with Half a Face

The next day a new guy came into the cell. Half his face was torn off, a single, smooth graft in its place.

Straight on, you understood he'd had some sort of accident—a fall onto the third rail or something. But the effect you got seeing his bad side as he lay on top his bunk was really eerie; in positioning himself to peer out the narrow window with his one eye, he left a smooth, featureless profile to the room.

On top of this, I don't think we ever spoke really. But he occupied my thoughts constantly. And each time I came into the room, he would be in the same place, whether asleep or awake, I couldn't tell.

Of course there were plenty of reticent fellows in prison. It was actually funny to hear the prison staff call out guys by their actual names, particularly when they'd gone by a street name for so long to protect themselves against informants. It seemed to give them a sort of physical discomfort. Other guys just wanted to talk. And it could be quite pleasant to lie in your bunk in the dark at night talking with your cellie. I remember Tray, for instance, who was positively spooked by the quiet of the south loop at night. And Keith who owned a chain of hairdressers around East St. Louis: a tall, elegant young man who liked to joke about how he was going to make his card partner wash his drawers. And Sam who was doing voodoo on his prosecutor. And Seth who used to exclaim "man, man, man, man, man" as prelude to his nightly recitation of his case.

But this was not the way with Kim. He just lay up in his bunk, a cipher. Perhaps that's emblematic of jail, where one is forever occupied with the mystery of one's fate, trying to piece together a riddle: Who tripped the alarm? Tipped off the cops? Ratted everybody out? And those last, unanswerable questions, the existential ones: *Will my girlfriend wait? Will my child know me when I get out? Will my parents be alive?*

If such thoughts went through Kim's mind, he didn't let on. Rather, he assumed the attitude of a condemned man, beyond hope or care and unwilling to satisfy his jailers with any apparent concern for the outcome: the Hamlet of Act V: *"If it be now, 'tis not to come; if it be not to come, it will be now; if it be not now, yet it will come: the readiness is all."*

Of course that's all conjecture. He was probably as scared shitless as the rest of us. Just his face didn't show it. And that's the problem. You want to know that men are men and bearing up under the pressure no better or worse than you are. And you can always tell. There's a false note in their boast. A trace of hysteria in their laughter.

It's there. Even the toughest cases. You read about them coming back on a "rule 35b" years later, deciding to cooperate after all.

I don't know what Kim's crime was. Robbing banks probably. He seemed like one of those downstate Illinoisans, heirs apparent to a particular Jesse James ethos. He was certainly cool enough. And he moved like smoke. Often I'd want to get back to the cell before him to establish my space. But he'd just be getting a leg up onto his top bunk as I opened the door. Or he'd slide in and get into the bunk before I could say a word. And that would be it.

The silence was palpable. And I began to conceive a dislike for the man. It was as if he were spiting me. And yet I was afraid of him; feared him.

I tried to imagine what the skin covering his right eye felt like. Cool and pink and fatty possibly. The porousness didn't quite match that of his face. It was taken from his thigh. And an odd thing, he had a boyish physique that contrasted with his marked, old man's face.

I found myself staring and felt ashamed, felt, strangely, that he knew I was watching him, which made me even more out of sorts.

Then one day he was gone, all his stuff cleared out except for his pillow, which kept the impression of his head.

I remember approaching it with fascination, the way you approached a bird's nest with eggs in it. I took the case off and looked at it for some time, then put the pillow under my own pillow and lay back in my bunk, sensing in the act an explanation of myself, of my own freedom and affliction.

But that's all wrong, of course—just the sort of foolish notion you take into your head in prison.

Soldiers with
Their Boots on

Everything seemed to come to a conclusion as far as I was concerned late in the fall of 1999. It was nothing out of the ordinary, really—just more jailhouse drama—but it was one of those instances when you suddenly see things that have taken up a disproportionate space in your imagination for all their smallness.

Let me begin with a definition and an etymology of sorts:

To steal on. Verb [intrans.] Informal. Chiefly Black American. To strike someone without warning—distinguished from *coldcock, blindside, sucker-punch* or other such *furtive* assaults—and most often formed past tense owing to its narrative affiliations, as in "He *stole on* that nigger."

I didn't know what this meant for some time. Then one cold November day on rooftop rec. the matter of definition was cleared up for me.

A bunch of us were sitting around waiting for the C.O. to let us back in. X and Y were playing a game of one-on-one. X, an apostate Latin King, but still just a kid, was backing Y down toward the hoop and really laying into him.

"What's up? What's up?" he said.

(Y was at a distinct disadvantage. He'd taken a 9MM bullet in the shin when the F.B.I. arrested him, apparently, and worn a cast for several months. He'd recently gotten the cast cut off and his leg looked pretty fucked up. So aside from sheer boredom there was a minor human-interest value.

Y was patiently trying to hold his ground, but X was roughly shouldering him toward the rim.

"What up?

My attention wandered off elsewhere.

"What up, bitch?"

There was sort of a pause, then a hollow thud, like if you thumped a watermelon. As I turned there was sort of a blur, and I thought maybe Y had punched the ball. Then I saw that hurt, sorrowful look in X's eye, and the redness on his jaw.

And someone said, "Oh shit, he stole on that nigger!"

Ah…. In time I came to realize that this wasn't so much about growing up in crime as growing up hard and Black and earnest and forthright. Of course I don't suppose that *every* guy that ever got stole on deserved it, but the great majority did.

Everything seemed to come to a conclusion, then, on one of those glorious fall afternoons on rooftop rec. The deco architecture of the South loop leaned inward. Sunlight danced up in the wires above the roof. A volleyball game of some little interest was being played. And for an hour or two you escaped from prison-boredom through joyful, childlike athletic effort.

Off in a corner, Frank "Nitty" Good slapped this boy from Gary, Indiana right upside his head.— I saw it in profile, a thing of real beauty: Frank rose right up onto his toes like a tennis player putting topspin on the ball and delivered a glancing, open-hand slap, and this fellow's face went all dark and he got real quiet.

Only afterwards did he start to make trouble. I was in my cell, when I heard a commotion outside.

"Frank Nitty slapped me like a bitch, dog. You can't just slap me like a beeyitch, dawg," the fellow implored. "You can't just slap me like a bitch, dog," he said again.

Frank just stood inside his doorway, not saying anything. Frank was a good guy—a nice guy, actually. You could see he'd been raised right, a son who said *Yes Ma'am* and *No Ma'am*. He was clean in his person, meticulous, in fact. He spoke politely. He was respectful. But he had a stubborn streak.

A bunch of guys from Gary, who seemed to have decided to organize themselves, impromptu, into a prison gang, stood around in the background. (The Feds had a treaty with the city of Gary, Indiana, authorizing them to make federal cases out of petty drug busts in order to clear the way for several Trump projects including casino boats and Miss America Pageant, rumor had it—a laudable if cynical goal, since "G.I." was by most accounts a dead mill town. As a consequence, there were a bunch of tall, skinny crack dealers, unkempt as tumble weeds, incarcerated at the Metropolitan Correction Center.)

Frank's cousin, Allgood, along with some other Black Disciples came running down into the hallway to even things out. Allgood stood almost a head taller than everyone else.

"You can't just slap me like a bitch, dog," the guy from Gary said, clearly warming to his lines.

"Well . . ." Allgood said, shrugging his shoulders as if to suggest the matter was settled.

"Ah, hell no!" the fellow from Gary said, beginning to pace back and forth. "You can't just slap me like a bitch, dog."

I admired his persistence. It was clear that he didn't want to fight, but he was being backed into a corner. He was aggrieved and he needed to save face.

Frank just leaned inside the frame of his door jutting out his jaw, and I imagined if there had been a spear of grass handy, he'd have broken it off and stuck it between his teeth.

Frank's cousin, Allgood, started his own pacing act, matching Gary in pitch and volume. "Hell, no. You can't just come down here," he said.

By now a crowd had started to form.

"Frank Nitty slapped me like a bitch, dog."

Allgood sniggered. He was a big, docile fellow who had recently become the object of our admiration when a segment of *COPS* featured him driving his fly-green corvette to O'Hare to lose a helicopter, later escaping through a hail of police gunfire with some fancy driving, only to be tracked down at a girlfriend's house later that night. When he came onto the unit we all cheered.

So when he got slapped around a day or two later by a wiry little Gary boy, it was quite a shock. The fight started in the day room and splintered off in two or three directions, with Allgood engaged in a running battle, retreating across the main floor, stunned, stopping to take an awkward swing, a girl-throw, and retreating again while the kid from Gary, clearly relishing the surprise himself, pursued with well-aimed punches to the back of Allgood's head.

Allgood sniggered, which seemed to set off Snake Carver, who had for some inexplicable reason inserted himself, again, in a situation that had absolutely nothing to do with him.

"I don't know what's wrong with this place," he started to yell. But Gary and Allgood were still yelling back and forth.

"You can't slap me like a bitch, dog."

"You can't just come up in here."

"Soldiers," Carver screamed, "lying in blood." This got everyone's attention.

"Soldiers with boots on."

I attempted a nervous laugh.

"Like a lot of *bitches* up in here. In the penitentiary, soldiers got their boots on. Soldiers lying in blood." Carver turned in my direction. "I don't know what you think this is."

For some reason the Latin Kings were in the hallway now, too, with their hands behind their backs, and I had the sudden sense that I'd gotten caught out in the open. I'd called attention to myself without knowing why or what for. I was trying to figure out what was up. Frank and them were *Folks,* the Latin Kings, *Peoples,* in Chicago gangland argot. The guys from Gary were … guys from Gary.

Snake Carver, as far as anyone could tell, was just an old-time con from L.A.—linked in my moral imagination with Jimmy Dharma like magnetic poles, equal and opposite, absolute and changeable.

… And I thought wistfully of Jimmy, who'd taught me to mind my own business and not look into guy's cells as I walked by, and to steer clear of crowds—he'd described how he once barged into a crowd of inmates out of curiosity just as a guy came lurching out of the scrum with a bloody shank.

Some kind of grudge was being played out, but I had no idea what it was. It seemed to me that everyone was waiting for everyone else to make the first move; it seemed to me this was the kind of dog that bit out of fear, and the longer nothing happened, the more likely it would happen.

Then Officer Newborn, who seemed to actually be paying attention for once, yelled for lockdown and hit the deuces on his radio to call for a response team.

For a few tense moments no one moved.

"Sheeit," the kid from Gary finally said.

"Shit," Allgood said.

And people started back toward their cells.

I took a deep breath—tried to act like everything was cool. Frank was already in his bunk, and I stood in the doorway next to Allgood, listening to the C.O. locking guys in on the tier. In the half-light of the jail, another day coming to an end, the two of us stood there, bound by some tacit agreement about this moment and our lives in general, and the things you wanted or didn't want, and the things happened or didn't happen, which hardly mattered anymore, which was the whole point.

"Fucking Carver, I said.

"Fucking Carver," Allgood said

"I shoulda stole on him," I said.

Y2K

They started messing with the environmental controls some time in December. Apparently the Bureau of Prisons had bought into the theory that at midnight on December 31, 1999 as the internal clocks rolled over to double-zero the computers were going to crash and the doors to the jails were going to pop open and inmates spill into the streets, erupting of course into a spontaneous orgy of raping, and stealing home electronics. So as a dry run they started powering down the jail, forcing us to breathe un-recycled air for hours at a time. I'm not sure what all this accomplished—the locking mechanisms on the unit doors were fired electronically, our cell doors were mechanical—other than interrupt a dozen games of computer solitaire no doubt going on in lonely precincts of the jail.

So on New Year's Eve they locked us in at 10 p.m., turned out the lights, and that as far as we were concerned was the *fin de siecle*.

The long-awaited millennium. For years you'd wondered where you'd be, where your life would take you: *Paris? The heights of Machu Pichu?* Of course New Year's Eve is the worst night of the year, anyway. Still, knowing in that cell what I hadn't known, couldn't have known all the years of my life, and all my unredeemed hopes....

So I lay there in the dark on the fifteenth floor of the Metropolitan Correction Center, listening to the radio. There was a cool program on: "Century to Century Jazz Party," broadcast live from venues around the country. They were at The Granite Room in New York, where they were just ringing in the new year. Then New Orleans. Then Oakland. I lay there listening, letting my mind drift out on the airwaves all across America. It was magical. It was beautiful, rising and falling with the music. Still a part of everything, though separated out. The mind darting out and darting back like a hummingbird.

As I think back to that hateful cell: sitting lotus at first light; lying in bed listening to the radio the night Mark McGuire broke the single-season home run record, a sultry night in the Midwest that transported you back a century to a time when baseball was played by men with pine tar on bare hands; and Christmas Eves, a gentle snow falling so quietly in the south loop, a thousand men, faces pressed against the windows like candles—as I think back to that cell, memories rise up as precious as ones from childhood ... because it's your life, after all, even if you have utterly and irrevocably gone and fucked it all up.

The first fireworks started to go off; I could hear them somewhere over the lake, and my eyes darted back and forth in the dark canyon of Van Buren Street until I caught a reflection of a reflection of a cascade of sparks. It reminded me of a fourth of July I'd spent stuck in a hotel waiting for Alhaji's call. I'd ordered room service and by the time the steak and half bottle got to my room, the fireworks had started; I could see them reflected in the building across the way as I sat there in my chair cutting and chewing, feeling entirely cut off from life....

I'd done it to myself, it was clear. In some way prison had only formalized that alienation.

Up on the fifteenth floor of MCC I lay in the dark, watching. A single laser shone a long, straight beam over State Street—a particle of light hurrying over the lake, the Midwestern darkness, pulling away from the earth's curvature and piercing the atmosphere, half way across the solar system already, and into eternity.

They were yelling into the toilets now. Guys who had "rappies" on other floors, or a cousin or a girlfriend or wife, had a system of communicating. You could empty the toilet bowl of water and yell down into the cell directly below yours. You could even yell from the fifteenth floor down to the twelfth where the women were. There were voices in the walls, repetitive, plaintive voices like someone calling after a lost dog. Guys would clean a toilet meticulously—though, you know, how clean can you ever really get jailhouse plumbing?—and stick their head right inside and start hollering away.

At about a quarter to twelve some guys started banging on the bars of their windows with their padlocks. At about five minutes before midnight the sound began to swell. The bars didn't ring; it was a dull, strangled sound. You'd hear it from time to time as someone decided to take out his frustration by giving the bars a few good raps. It is a sound fitted to that place. A sound that could exist nowhere else on earth. Now the inmates began beating on those bars in a collective rage and stupidity and joy. The cops, ordinarily so ready to quell any kind of emotional display, were helpless, and for minutes on end we beat on the bars, an unabashed *fuck you,* a cry to be saved.

Escape(ism)

I woke to a commotion—the sound of lockers flipping over.

"Don't do it," someone shouted.

You could hear pounding on a door below. Shouting from within the cells. The unit door buzzed and then banged open.

The story was pieced together later in the gym, where they evacuated us. One relatively new fellow, a tall, quiet kid, an Army veteran, was running around the unit tearing shit up. All night long, and perhaps for several days, he'd been digging away at the concrete around his window. He'd managed to pry the steel grate free and knock out the window and had been chipping frantically away at the concrete, trying to make an opening wide enough to slip through. All night he'd been trying to wriggle through, his torso raw and bleeding from the effort.

He must have given up when the sun came up and sat there now in the middle of his cell, shivering in the cold winter air, unable to put things right: a rope of knotted sheets and improvised climbing harness scattered on the floor. And when the C.O., a little military girl whose husband was a hack too, came and unlocked the door, he snapped and shoved the door open, sending her stumbling back into the hall.

He was on her in an instant. A short right cross to the jaw sent her sprawling on the floor.

"Don't do it," someone yelled.

The inmate kicked her walkie-talkie off the tier, and continued his rampage. He picked up his foot locker and ran out onto the tier and hurled it over the edge, the sheet metal box landing in a thunderous crash. Tipped over the bunk bed. Then he ran down onto the main floor and upended the C.O.'s desk. He threw some chairs around. In all, it didn't seem like there was much damage one could do, yet his fury seemed to escalate by the minute. He was up by the counselor's offices tearing down bulletin boards. He smashed a phone. Set off a sprinkler.

Then all of a sudden an acrid smell filled the air, and a smoky haze. The front door fired and a response team ran in. The inmate retreated to the second tier followed by a cop in heavy armor. Inmate let off a long chemical spray from a fire extinguisher, obscuring the cop's view. Undaunted, the cop charged through the haze and got knocked on the pate by the blunt end of the extinguisher and went down in a heap. More cops charged, and the inmate let off another blast and retreated farther up the steps. They were hemming him in, but he kept them at bay for minutes on end, which infuriated the cops. Every moment they failed to control the situation was a deep affront to their sense of mission. The extinguisher exhausted, the inmate finally hurled it at the cops which sent them scrambling. Recovering themselves, the cops set upon the inmate like dogs, kneeling on his neck, twisting arms, standing on his ankles and hands. The fight was out of him now, and he went limp as the cops carried him bodily to the hole.

Later they had us down in the gym, sitting on the floor like POWs. They had to submit us; they couldn't have it any other way. Then I saw the C.O.'s husband doing a pantomime at the far end of the gym, making like his hands were cuffed behind his back, then wham-wham, left, right. We never saw that kid again.

Endgame

Of course Carver and I became cellies after all. Whatever enmity existed between us only drew us together.

He seemed pleased with my progress as a convict. I'd endured physical hardships on the dip bar. I'd listened to his rants. He stood there grinning as I hauled my legal box and an assortment of books and commissary up the short flight of stairs onto the tier.

In truth we probably affirmed each other's worse instincts....

The cell was meticulous, sterile might be a more apt description. The bed was made with a military precision, counter top wiped down, floor waxed to a dull sheen. It was a thing I'd noticed from time to time—the way inmates tried to eradicate the presence of anything, even themselves, from their cells. If Carver had family somewhere, there was no evidence of it; no picture of wife or mother by the bedside; just a little photo album he kept in his foot locker.

Carver buried himself in legal work. He was pursuing a medical malpractice claim against the BOP. "They fucked my brain up," he said. "I got a bloody brain. I got it documented right here," he said, tapping the legal box under his bed, which he never let out of his site. Whether he was on the main floor working out or playing chess or eating, he kept the box in his line of site. He didn't go to the gym, and when he went to the law library he'd deputize somebody to watch his room. It was his best hope, a passed pawn. He was playing to win. Except the queening square was always protected one way or another. No plea deal came. No favorable ruling from the judge. He sent out motion after motion which the judge summarily dismissed.

"They know it," he said. "They know it."

I had no doubt that Carver was a criminal. And I also had no doubt that they'd fucked him up somehow and were simply going to let him die in prison. He must have known it too. The knowledge of that burned down inside him a long, cool flame of hatred. Only occasionally the flame guttered. "I got a bloody brain," he hollered.

He never asked me about my crime. A convict has a delicate sensibility in that regard. He only wanted to know that I was un-reconciled with my jailers. For him there was no other way, rightly so. At the very least one did not cooperate....

My time was running down at MCC, and I was just plain tired of it all. And slipping. So when Carver asked me to edit some legal work one afternoon and I actually said No, I was busy with my own stuff, it didn't take long for the honeymoon to end. I was brushing my teeth and accidentally spit into the sink, which we kept clean for icing leftovers, when Carver blew up.

"You just spit in the sink?" he said.

"Oh, shit. I didn't mean to," I said.

"We put our food in there."

"I know."

"Why'd you spit in the sink?"

"I didn't mean to."

"You know what? You got a problem now."

I stood there, speechless.

"I got a bloody brain," he said, crossing the cell toward me.

"I didn't mean it," I said.

He took his glasses off. "You know what? I want you to clean that shit up," he said, his anger flaring like a match. "I want you to clean up the whole sink. And when I get back from the library if that's sink's not clean, then you're going to feel a black man's rage."

Of course one has to deal with one's share of indignities in prison, but they're generally of an anonymous, institutional variety. This was personal.

I considered what would happen if I left the sink. We'd fight, I supposed. Carver definitely had jail strength, the kind of isometric strength you develop pushing back for decades against implacable realities of jail. But the real problem was the first move was his—unless one wanted to make some sort of preemptive maneuver, which I realized I couldn't do, whether because I liked Carver and couldn't envision fighting him, or because I had bigger problems, or because I was afraid. And this is what separated me from so many other men in prison and why I would never be quite re-spected there.

I went back and forth with the thing a few times, then made a few half-hearted swipes at the sink with some paper towels.

That seemed to appease Carver when he got back from the law library. But things had changed.

"You want me to look at your motion," I asked later.

"No, that's alright," he said.

Sentence

On the day of my sentencing, I sat in the bullpen, three typewritten sheets folded neatly in thirds in the breast pocket of my jumpsuit. A dozen souls dozed lightly in late morning sunlight filtering through the window shades.

At some point we were woken by the bullpen door clanging open as a couple of guys stomped into the cell on their way back from court. There was brief cursing. Then they didn't say any more. I sat there, groggy, waiting for lunch.

Eventually some warder came down the hall and wheeled in food. I ate a Bologna sandwich and some potato chips and drank a soda. Then I sat and waited some more.

Around two P.M. the door at the end of the hall opened and two United States Marshalls in jackets and ties came and got me and led me into the courtroom, a big ceremonial-looking room with high ceilings and light the color of weak tea.

My lawyer, Sean, was standing at the defendant's table. Behind him, in the first row of the gallery, were my mother and father. AUSA MacBride and Agents Brett and Wayne were at an adjacent table. A stenographer and a court reporter sat against the wall.

I shook hands with Sean and smiled at my parents. Then I turned around to face the bench. I'd been in this courtroom at least a dozen times, but it looked different today.

"United States of America versus Nicholas Fillmore, Jr., the Honorable Judge Norgle presiding," the bailiff called out. "All rise."

Judge Norgle, a Reagan-appointee with a sober face, came briskly through the chamber door adjusting the sleeves of his robe and settled himself at the bench.

The principles identified themselves, and Judge Norgle addressed me directly.

"Do you understand the charges being proffered against you?"

"Yes, I understand them, Your Honor," I said, feeling like I'd spoken too much.

"Do you understand you have pleaded guilty?"

"Yes, sir."

"Have you read the court's pre-sentence investigation report?"

I said I had.

Did I have any objections?

"No."

Then he asked if I had anything to say.

I stepped up to the lectern and unfolded my sheets of paper and began to read. As he always did, Judge Norgle stared right through me. When I was finished, I folded up the papers and put them back in my pocket. Then Sean spoke. Then the Judge asked if anyone else had anything to say, and my parents stepped forward as Sean held the gallery gate for them.

In the cavernous theater of the courtroom, amidst the spectacle of the law, and the machinery of the law, we suddenly seemed small parts—frightened, small-town people whose son had gotten in trouble.

My mother spoke briefly, spreading her manicured hands in front of her and looking at her engagement ring, her wedding band, her mother's opal ring as if summoning a collective wisdom, a faint, violent shaking of her head.

Then my father spoke a few sentences. "I know Marines aren't supposed to cry," he said, choking up.

The room was silent for a moment. Then the judge called on the Prosecutor. This was what it all came down to.

AUSA MacBride actually spoke glowingly of me, lauding me for my cooperation. "Mr. Fillmore has done everything asked of him. He has answered all our questions. He has remained incarcerated at the Metropolitan Correction Center for the last four years." I looked up now and smiled as kindly as I could after she finished her recitation. Then the Judge began shuffling papers, wrapped in thought.

"I am not unmoved," he said, still looking down, "but this is a serious offense, and the court needs to impress upon the defendant the seriousness of the offense."

"Oh-oh," I thought. Any wayward hope of "time served" dashed on the rocks, I listened carefully now, like someone tuning a radio to some distant signal late in the night. And here it came between little bursts of static. "I sentence the defendant to 94 months incarceration, to be served at a camp close to defendant's home district, along with participation in the 500 hour Residential Drug and Alcohol Program."

The Marshalls moved in, too quickly as always, and began escorting me to the door. I turned to my parents. "I'm sorry," I said.

As the Marshalls were unlocking the door that led back to the bullpen, Sean, was talking with animation, filling the awful void and explaining to my parents that with time already served and time off for the 500 hour drug program, and time off for good behavior, I really only had a few years more, close to home, in the relative safety and sanity of a federal prison camp. AUSA MacBride, too, had gone over to offer words of encouragement. A few years. Still, a lifetime.

The next day I was in my cell. Someone came up to me: "man, you're in the paper," he said; then he disappeared. So I held my breath and sought out a copy. Sure enough, there it was on page three of the City section of the Tribune.

A narrow account of my allocution, the article recounted stuff designed for the ears of people in court, certainly not my prison mates. It mentioned my parents; talked about a "day of reckoning"; endeavored, in so many words, to make me out to be a white boy caught in a black man's trap. And it formally outed me as a rat.

I don't know if you've ever run a gauntlet before. Though nobody said anything, it was like ducking your head under invisible blows.

In fact, nobody seemed to notice at all. Except Snake Carver, on the rail grinning at me. But that was it. People had their own problems. And I was on my way out the door.

Back at Square One

When they told me to pack out, the joy—the soaring joy—that I felt was foregrounded by a painful self-reflection: the next morning as the C.O. called my name and I walked to the main floor and the unit door fired and I stepped tentatively into the hallway toward the elevators and glanced back at those inmates up early and standing on the rail, ghosts of myself; as I made my way through R&D, shuffled down the hallway into the sally port and got on the transport with half a dozen other prisoners; and as the steel door rolled up revealing the light of day and the bus hurtled into traffic turning not toward Dirksen but onto the highway, and it became clear that *Yes, I was leaving* ... something lifted and momentarily freed of conscience I was struck by a glimpse of myself I had not seen in four years, and I felt unutterably sad for all that I had lost.

*

The Marshall's flight took us from Chicago back to Oklahoma City, and for the next week I did nothing but eat and sleep and take slow, slow walks around the unit, a large, single-tiered dorm with cells around the outside. A single Corrections officer sat at a desk in a sunken control area at the center of the room.

At four o'clock lock-down I fell into my bunk, psychically exhausted. My cellie rattled the bunk before the C.O. got there, and I jumped to my feet for count. Then I fell back into my bunk and into a narcotic-like slumber, my cellie rousing me again— *"La comida,"* he said, sweetly, after the C.O. had unlocked the door.

My second week I met this Israeli named Eitan who was headed to Otisville, like I was. A lot of Jewish guys got sent there because they had a rabbi. I was just a rat, and so the judge did me the favor of sending me to a cushy camp near home. Eitan was headed to the medium security.

We played cards for squats, roped new guys into the game. Really busted ass. The next morning we saw this guy in his early fifties who'd been moping around the place; they'd captured him after twenty years on the lam, and he was kind of putting himself out there as far as talking about his case with everyone and anyone and generally doing things contrary to the convict way, and so Eitan and I took it upon ourselves to straighten him out—we saw this guy taking baby steps down the stairs, kind of sliding off the edge of each riser, his Achilles tendons seized up, his quads so fucked he couldn't bend his knees, and Eitan and I were laughing so hard.

"I think we overdid it," he said, tears welling up in his eyes.

Finally we got loaded back onto the plane, and I was looking out the window, no idea where we were headed, when all of a sudden I realized we were curving low over the Miami coastline. Now you have to understand: after being locked up inside, the mere *idea* of the world laid out thus tried one's credulity, forget gliding through light and air and element of the south Florida coast.

We landed on some kind of service runway built on a landfill at the back of the airport and picked up prisoners from MCC Miami, then we were back in the air, briefly, before landing in the pine suburbs of Atlanta. Then they drove us inside the wall and into the heart of darkness: Atlanta United States Penitentiary.

It wasn't so bad at first. They gave us bologna sandwiches and coca cola. We were sitting in the visiting area, in open air, a summer's day coming to and end. Then they marched us down a ramp and into a subterranean maze of hallways shut off from the light. I couldn't help thinking of the pens beneath the floor of the Roman Coliseum. Apparently this was the transfer wing—at one time the hole. A real slave ship.

The place was illumined by a weak, yellowish light like those old bug lights in summer. And for a moment I thought wistfully of the Dairy Queen near our apartment when I was just a child, 1966 maybe—one of the earliest memories of my life—standing there with my dad, who must have been in his twenties still: my dad, possessed of all that brutal tenderness only those whose lives have been redeemed by the birth of a child, a son, can understand.

Everybody was locked behind steel doors. There were no sounds. No sensation of air moving. No phone calls. No mail call. No rec. No law library. No one even knew you were here. It was like being buried alive.

They put me into a cell. Some guy was asleep on the bottom bunk, so I climbed up to the top. Shortly after another guy came in. The guard closed the door, and the guy was left standing there in the middle of the floor in the dark. There was no bed for him. No chair. I threw my blanket down to him. He'd have to make do on the floor.

Since there was no window in the door, no window to the outside, no clock or radio, you could only guess what was going on outside: the time of day, when the next meal was coming, whether the world still existed.

I slept fitfully, waking several times, convinced it was mid-morning and the transport had taken off and I'd be left there for good. I didn't think that I could take it. Even after everything I went through at MCC, nothing prepared you for this kind of privation. Doors opening and closing echoed down imagined hallways. The sound of a shower. I waited for the key to hit the lock. Still nothing. Now I was sure I'd missed the transport.

A bare light bulb burned overhead. The cement blocks were painted grey-brown. The paint on the bunks was battered, chips of blue, white and red flecking the iron. You had the feeling in a cell that there was no surface that hadn't been worried over, rubbed, gouged, sweat upon. Men's spirits had been broken in this room. The ghosts of their despair still beat on the walls.

Suddenly the door opened and the guard called one of the other guy's names. Then he closed the door. *Fuck!* There was nothing to do but to close your eyes, block it all out, try to sleep.

Finally they came and got you and your heart was racing to get out of there. It was that way with everyone. One guy was in such a hurry he stumbled into a guard while pulling on his shoe. Several guards rushed over, roughed the guy up and dragged him back inside. We didn't see him on the flight.

The plane made it back to New York in astonishingly short time, and suddenly I was standing on the tarmac at Stewart Airport where I'd stood in the rain four years earlier, swearing I'd make it back. I wasn't home yet, not nearly, but had passed through some nadir.

We piled into a little bus and drove up route 84 into the foothills of the Catskills where Otisville Federal Prison sits atop a hill in the Shawangunk range. The bus took us behind the fence of the medium security, FCI. As we were processed in, they removed our cuffs and gave us prison-issue greens. Everyone, except me, was herded through a door to the medium security facility. I took one last look at them: castaways, knees braced against the thwarts, riding into the waves.

I was left sitting placidly on a bench. Ten minutes later a jovial guard showed up and we got into an SUV and drove outside the fence and up a little hill to a cluster of pre-fab metal dormitories, and a most miraculous thing happened: he let me out of the car and said, "Ok, go check in with the C.O." Then he drove away, leaving me standing outside in a clearing in the fading twilight, heady fragrances of a summer evening swimming all around me.

What followed was no less miraculous. I was shown to a small dorm. Out back Joe Lee, Lenny Bello and Scotty Boombatz were leaning back in their chairs against the wall and smoking cigars under the pines. Joe pulled a cigar out of his shirt pocket and handed it to me. "Welcome to Club Fed," he said. "Have a cigar."

Club Fed

Joe Lee landed me a job working on grounds crew, this older Chinese fellow from Brooklyn. On my first day, we cruised around in a propane powered golf cart watering shrubs. This took about an hour. We spent the rest of the afternoon basically joy-riding the winding "Two-Mile Drive" that led up to Otisville camp. Each morning when we checked in Joe concocted some kind of chore for us, and the shop foreman, Tony, basically played along. Next day we took "the mule" to the bottom of Two-Mile Drive and lay back in tall grass staring up at the trees.

"Keep your weed whacker running," Joe said. "Tony'll come and feel the motor, and if it's cold he'll know you've been fucking off."

Back at the dorms, Scotty Boombatz was encamped on the south side of the dorm, taking in the sun; his Ray-Ban Aviators and Montecristo no. 2 were definitely not commissary-issue.

Paul Mavros and Doc Stevens were hitting tennis balls on the "court," a net at the top of the visitor's parking lot, which slanted down and to the right, so you basically towered above your opponent, though your volleys quickly overshot the base line.

Gregg Rudog was hunting for crystals in the dirt below the woods. It was so hot you could hear the pinecones cracking open in sunlight.

Most other inmates were working at the power plant or behind the fence at the medium security facility. The few inmates that had managed to scam jobs as orderlies hung around the dorms all day—old men fallen from grace, enervated by the heat and boredom and the effort to hold their stories together.

Gene, the President of a community college on Long Island, caught fooling with financial aid, had the endearing habit of scrambling to his feet to receive anyone who entered the little dorm. By degrees his formal manners abandoned him till he merely sprawled in his bunk in a T-shirt, reading potboilers.

Doc was convicted of defrauding Medicare. Paul was in for bid-rigging. The list went on and included crimes I couldn't understand. What became clear, though, was that the thieves—the *gonefs*—seemed to inhabit one half of the main dorm, the drug dealers the other half, each affecting a vague moral distaste for the other—the drug dealers themselves divided uneasily between those who took their ten or twenty years on the chin and worked their way down to a camp and those who'd opted for the shortcut: ratting out their co-defendants.

I thought briefly of Alhaji, who was incarcerated in less congenial surroundings, no doubt, in his own English MCC. I wondered what artful dodgers, skinheads and Jamaican drug posses he must be locked up with. How he managed without his connections. You relied on yourself then. And for a moment I could almost picture him in some stooped law library, contending amongst a group of inmates, a Pakistani, a fellow Nigerian, over the fine points of international extradition law and the EU Convention on Human Rights. Then the image would fade.

It was Saturday night and I was looking for a place to hang. In the law library a lot of Hasids were watching the Yankee game, presided over by Sol, a fellow of infinite personality and physical stature. His crime, too, was of a certain magnitude. It was raucous fun, but my heart alas does not reside in the Bronx.

A lot of guys were watching a movie in the visiting room. I was too antsy.

Joe and Scotty and Lenny were smoking behind the dorm. Maybe later.

The black inmates were watching BET in the trailer in front of the dorm, (and there's a funny story I won't tell, weeks later, about a skunk, a raccoon and a loaf of white bread—in the ensuing stink guys falling all over each other to get out the trailer door.)

Beyond the trailer, in a little clearing bright with moonlight and stars, a half-mile walking track skirted the woods. The sound of cicadas rose into the cool night air of August and I started out walking, one lap, then another, joy rising in my chest with each deep breath of the woods, rich and rank and organic. Ten laps. I couldn't seem to get enough. After all those years in Chicago breathing stale, re-circulated air, I couldn't seem to exist in this rarefied atmosphere.

Twenty laps.

A trans-Atlantic flight heading into JFK blinked far off in the night sky, a glistening jelly stirring with life.

Thirty laps.

At last I quit, headed back into the dorm and lay back on my bunk, listening to the sounds of a hundred men or more breathing in the dark.

Pretty soon I had a routine: work, then dinner, then work out for an hour or so with Rudog, (before smoking). There was a lovely little Quonset hut with free weights. After four years of makeshift workouts in MCC, of endless pull-ups, dips, squats, at last I had access to the coveted free weights. Between daily workouts and protein-rich diet I was knocking the ball into the trees in left field with ease and letting go throws that made the seams of the ball hiss. Finally I reached some pointless goal: I was ready to try for 225; and I said, finally, as Jimmy Dharma joked all those years ago—as I'd waited to say all those years knowing it meant that freedom was imminent—I said to Rudog, "Throw another wheel on, Holmes." He laughed and said, "What?" And I said, "Put another *plate* on the bar, *Holmes*," and he got it and put another couple 45 pound weights on the bar, and I lay back and let my breathing get real shallow, and slowly built it up, marshaling all my concentration on lifting the bar off the rack and driving it past that point, and locking it out….

Dr. Bamboo

One afternoon agents Brett and Wayne and another agent on the extradition case against Alhaji showed up at the camp.

They'd commandeered the law library and brought me in there in my sweats and baseball glove. A number of inmates looked at me askance, and I could hear the beehive humming with the news. *Fuck it.*

They had the tape recording of my conversation with Alhaji the day of my arrest back in New York and wanted to smooth out the transcription; whoever did the job had me talking like a tough and had misconstrued one thing after another.

It seems the Feds had been unable to establish Alhaji's identity.

"Did I pick the wrong guy?" I asked, referring to the photo lineup back in Chicago.

"You didn't pick Alhaji, no."

"No?"

"No. It's complicated. He's claiming his identical brother is the one who's the heroin smuggler. It's a mess. You can't get any reliable documentation out of Nigeria," Agent Wayne said charitably.

This sounded entirely like Alhaji: moving in several different directions at once: at the same time he claimed that his brother was the actual "Alhaji," he claimed that he had personally worked as an informant for drug enforcement in Benin and Togo, and was now claiming that he had information concerning the American Embassy bombing in Kenya as well as the planning of 9-11, gleaned, I supposed, in Brixton Prison.

He'd actually beaten a preliminary extradition motion, only to be rearrested and charged at the request of the American government. Now his lawyers were making hay of the fact American prosecutors had failed to disclose my misidentification.

I'd blown it, not intentionally, of course, but how did anyone know that for sure? (How did I even know for sure?) The Feds could revoke my 5k1 agreement at any time and use the material I'd furnished against me. Haul me right back to Chicago.

Yet it all seemed so trivial. Didn't they know I had a ballgame that afternoon? That I'd slipped from their grasp already? was running beneath a deep fly ball in the outfield grass, sure of my route, my life beginning again?

Of course the episode was a forceful reminder, over my objections, how I was really at their service in the end, the phrase "never-ending relationship" echoing in memory.

Autumn arrived and we relished the final warm days before cold weather locked us in. One evening during the Chinese Mid-Autumn Festival, Joe Lee and I walked out on the lawn to look up at the full moon—an ancient tradition involving family reunions, partings and sorrow.

I thought about L. Now that I was safely tucked away, now that I was safe, she could let go.

I'd called her up. Our phone conversations were exceedingly rare. Besides being expensive (and collect), there was a quixotic quality to jailhouse calls; and visits. I wrote every day instead. (Somewhere there's a envelope full of letters, which I'm afraid to look at for their dead earnestness.)

"How are you?" I asked.

"Fine."

"What's happening?"

"Nothing."

"Where are you staying?"

"An apartment."

"Where?"

"Waikiki."

The conversation continued like that; forced.

"What's the matter?"

"Nothing."

"You seem like you don't want to talk."

"Not really."

"Oh," I said.

"I don't want you thinking that we're together."

"I don't," I said.

"I don't want any expectations."

"Okay," I said.

"That I'm waiting."

"Alright," I said.

"How are you?" she said after a minute."

Maybe I knew all this already, but it staggered me, and I walked around bleary-eyed for a day. I couldn't afford to indulge in any cheap theatrics, though. I knew she was out there somewhere—far away on a Pacific trade wind, circling....

Already preparations were being made for winter: plastic put up on windows, snow blowers serviced, a night-time volunteer snow removal crew put together. The inmates, too, began laying in supplies for the winter. Boombatz seemed to have caches of cigars hidden in all the ceilings. An older Iranian fellow had a yogurt culture under his bed.

Family visited. We had real Chinese food from Chinatown smuggled in. I walked the track while Joe visited with his family and when I sensed no one was looking plucked a bag out of the open window of a car parked on the edge of the track, stuck it under my sweatshirt and walked into the dorm to hide it for later.

Then one day shortly after Thanksgiving the C.O. told me to pack out, they'd processed my transfer to Allenwood Camp for the drug and alcohol program.

I was a little bit heartbroken leaving Joe. I couldn't say why exactly. Maybe we fulfilled some familiar role for each other: brother, uncle, *lao-shi,* or knew each other in some previous life, or maybe we just felt the simple bonhomie of men who had come through an ordeal and found ourselves in the same lifeboat.

There were flurries in the air as I walked through camp, past the dorms and the ball field and the shop, back toward the Medium, the way I'd come in months earlier. On the hill behind me the life of the camp went on in its cozy way.

I put my head down and trudged along the perimeter road of the FCI to the front entrance and rang the buzzer to R&D. They let me inside and locked me in a holding cell. Then they strip-searched me and dressed me in khakis and put handcuffs and shackles on me and loaded me on the little armored bus. Along the ride I thought of the famed meeting between Li Po and Tu Fu: "I met Tu Fu on a mountaintop / in August when the sun was hot. Under the shade of his big straw hat / his face was sad."

*

That night I was back inside Brooklyn MDC. My head ached from caffeine withdrawal. I suppose I'd gotten older in the four years since I was here last because the open dorm felt like recess; it was kids everywhere with irrepressible kid-energy—happiness almost. I burrowed under my blanket and fell asleep. Then some ridiculous noise woke me up and I jumped down off my bunk and staggered to the row of stalls against the wall and puked into a toilet. Since I had no shower shoes I grabbed a trash bag and brought it into the shower to stand on, the water all running into the drain at my feet.

Two weeks later they loaded us onto a bus for Pennsylvania. We stopped at MCC Philadelphia, and some guy got on and sat next to me. Before long he started talking. They'd just fetched him out of the hole and he seemed a little starved for conversation. They kept him locked up wherever he went. He was an escape artist.

The bus pulled off the interstate so the cops could get McDonalds, and we sat in bright winter sunlight talking.

"Alright, how would you bust out of this van, for instance?" I asked.

He looked around for a second. It was an armored two-ton truck with wire mesh over all the windows and a mesh door across the front. "I'd go into the bathroom and see if I could rip the toilet off the floor. You could probably get enough leverage to do that. And then if I could fit through the hole in the floor I'd try to bust through the reservoir; it's probably plastic and you could either bust a hole in it or crack a seam."

I looked over at him. He was slender, delicate almost, his pale skin like that of some cave-dwelling creature, his eyes the strangest blue-green, I thought, from peering down avenues of escape.

"The trick," he said, "is to find a weakness, a weld or seam and keep at it ... because whatever has a way in has a way out."

As the truck rolled into Western, Pennsylvania and the day deepened, he told me of his exploits. He'd busted out of a USP and become the object of a multi-state manhunt—I could look it up and see. He'd escaped somewhere a second time, remained obdurate in his refusal to comply with the terms of his incarceration. I'd met other guys like this—Snake Carver was one—whom you could revere like saints, who were saintly in their unwavering commitment to an ideal.

We got a little peekaboo of USP Lewisburg as we dropped off some guys there, the long drive past the front gate leading in dramatic fashion to the gothic facade of the central tower. In the shadow of the brick wall you felt like a sapper making an assault on a medieval castle.

From there it was a short drive to Allenwood Prison. First we stopped off at the medium security, where I was kind of hinting I was headed, not wanting to tell Escape Artist I was headed to camp. It didn't feel like that. It felt like I'd done time. When they didn't call my name, I tried to play it off. "Hmm," I said. At the camp I feigned surprise.

"Ah, you're a lucky guy," he said.

They got me and another guy through R&D pretty fast. It was clear by the cops' demeanor that this was no Otisville, though. After the usual processing, they sent me to my dorm. The main part of the camp was a group of low brick buildings (used as ordinance depots during WWII), set on a slight incline below a thin stretch of woods. The buildings—three dorms, a library, a gym, a dining hall and some kind of facilities building—were all connected, each to the other, by a series of sidewalks, a cement wheel; not a good sign. The yard was empty; they were all in the dorms waiting to be let out for dinner; you could see inmates bunched up in the lobbies. What were they all doing now back at Otisville? I wondered and trudged toward the dorm with a sigh.

Rounding Third

The first thing to do was to get a job to put yourself out of sight, particularly at a place like Allenwood with its rules—no feeding the geese, shirt tucked in, no towel on the bunk.

Given the choice between the medium security, the "treatment plant" and education, I sauntered over to Ed Smitty's little GED classroom in the library basement.

Inmates dressed in khaki trousers and shirts sat in rows at their desks working over problems in books. Ed Smitty sat at his desk at the back of the class, a nice, ineffectual man glancing longingly through the BOP website at the ad for Education Specialist at Honolulu MDC.

I gave Smitty an oral summary of my vita, and he told me I was hired. "Come back tomorrow," he said.

In the far corner of the room, a couple guys at the tutor's table looked up from their reading and smiled. Next day Smitty introduced me to my colleagues: Bob White, a Yalie, and another fellow.

"Welcome," Bob White said, extending his hand.

"Thanks. So what's the routine here?"

"Well, basically we sit at this table and when you feel like giving a lesson you tell Smitty."

This was to be my refuge until my turn came for the 500-hour drug treatment program and the softball season rolled around in the spring. For eight hours a day I'd be burrowed into the corner, reading, murmuring to my colleagues and nodding asleep after lunch—along with a dozen other inmates, and Smitty himself, in the long, stultifying afternoons ... until Booby, a jovial three-hundred-pound Dominican, would yell *BANGIN!* and everybody would lurch forward in his seat wiping drool off his chin, and Smitty would say, exasperated, *"Booby!"*

Bob White gave a math lesson on my first day. I admired the thoroughness of his presentation. He used a large ruler and graph to demonstrate negative and positive integers. Bob was a lecturer in psychology at Yale—that is until he got caught borrowing social security numbers. In his defense, he had extravagant tastes; and he was still in the closet.

We got to be friends and maintained an arch sense of humor about things, which lifted us out of the daily misery of prison life.

"Call the sommelier; this bottle is off," he said, holding his bug juice to the light.

After a little while I conceived the idea to teach *Hamlet*. I suppose that teaching Shakespeare was ambitious, but I felt like giving something of myself, and my ambition, dormant for so long, needed rousing.

Following Bob's lead, I ironed my uniform, combed my hair, and endeavored to comport myself like a scholar. Smitty stepped to the front of the class, said I would be teaching *Hamlet* and told them to pay attention.

I stepped up to the dry-erase board and looked around. Ayala, an innocent-seeming Dominican guy, looked up earnestly, pencil in hand, ready to take notes. Castro, a short, scarred fellow, sat back in his chair and folded his arms across his chest. A couple guys in back murmured between themselves.

"Why bother with Shakespeare?" I asked. "Besides being the greatest poet of the English language, no other writer challenges us as Shakespeare does to consider what it means to be human…. Anyway, if you can understand Shakespeare, the reading comprehension section of the GED test will be a breeze," I said, a little abashed.

Of course, "Denmark is a prison." Hamlet's mad antics are familiar to any convict, accused by events. For to be wrong, to be deprived of one's very reasons, is intolerable.

We began to slowly read the play aloud, alternating parts, stopping here and there to explicate. Guys were mostly cooperative out of a desire to do something besides work through exercises in a book. Then Castro decided he'd had enough and began groaning, murmuring and generally expressing discontent. A few others joined him, and suddenly I had the makings of a full-scale rebellion on my hands.

I had no idea what to do. I thought of ways I might show up Castro in class, dwelling more on my bruised ego than the problem at hand.

"You've got to talk to Castro outside of class," Bob White said. "Once you lose a class, you can never get it back."

I thought about it and decided it was the only way. I spent the evening thinking about Castro. He was about five-six, had iron grey hair and a deep scar, which ran down his forehead and branched impossibly on the side of the nose and across his cheek. It was hard to look at, hard to untangle from the deep, tanned lines of his face.

At the end of the next day as everyone was getting ready to leave I went up to him and asked if we could talk for a minute.

"Yeah?" he said.

"Look, I just want you to know that I'm on your side. I only want to help you guys get your GED. I'm sorry if I came across wrong," I said, struggling to make eye contact.

"Oh, yeah," Castro said. "I can appreciate that. That's cool."

And that was the end of it. I had an ally now in Castro, who'd only wanted to be consulted—who felt, rightly, that I'd barged in without proper feeling.

So we continued with Hamlet, reading, playing parts and comparing our dramatic interpretations with the ready violence of the Mel Gibson movie version. I remember the last day, diagramming the slaughter and thinking how the lines describe a John Woo shootout as much as anything, and feeling a momentary sense of victory as I crossed off names of the *dramatis personae,* (pleased in the way one is pleased at making a credible interpretation of a work of art), then a chill of recognition as Fortinbras ponders the unnatural state of affairs, the terrible waste of talent and youthful vigor.

Line Drive

Winter dragged on into spring, which arrived rather gloriously in the Alleghenies. Canada geese came in droves. Frost thawed and ground water welled up in footprints. Big wads of cloud piled high into a pastel blue sky. And one day a cartful of baseball mitts showed up in the gym.

Of course there's no sweeter labor in spring than working in a glove. The act of oiling and rubbing and pounding it with your fist and popping the ball into that leather till it's broken in is an act of devotion.

The middle infielder wants to take the ball hot off the palm, so he's always bending the middle fingers inward to make the glove fan out. It's like trying to comb a new part in your hair. It won't stay. Throw it down and it folds back along the hinge. And so an infielder is an obsessive-compulsive type, tirelessly shaping and reshaping his glove, constantly rehearsing the act, felt long into old age, of corralling a ground ball and delivering it in a fluid motion to first.

I sorted through the pile and took possession of something workable and secreted it back to my bunk.

The next day I threw the ball around behind the gym with Dominican Ayala. The first day out you try to take it easy. Anyone will tell you that throwing a ball overhand is an unnatural motion. Adrenaline, however, gets the better of you, and suddenly you're firing the ball around like its July 4th.

Ayala whipped one at me and I got the middle finger of my throwing hand caught in the glove, and the ball nailed me on the tip of the bone, sending a thrilling pain into my wrist. You know you're hurt when the thing is still killing you an hour later. Instead of that nice warm feeling, it got more and more tender. Later the nail turned black and fell off.

The next day tryouts started. It was cold and windy like every other tryout since I was seven years old. Baseball begins at the equinox, its proper image not crowds and high skies and bunting hung from upper decks ... but old men with windbreakers pushed up on cord-like forearms smacking fungos, one after another, at reticent infielders.

Mr. Ransom, a hack, was perpetually pissed off. Whiskey-sotted, a wad of chaw in his cheek, deer blood under his fingernails, he inspired a kind of love. I have played ball for humpbacks, megalomaniacs, brawlers. The more depraved, the better. Every good coach has something of Ahab about him.

Ransom yelled "bring it home" and hit a two-hopper at me. I charged and more or less blocked it with my glove—I had no feel for the ball with the bruised finger on my throwing hand—and got hold of it finally and came up side arm, the ball tailing right at Ransom's head.

"Jesus H. Christ," he yelled, ducking out of the way with a dexterity that surprised me.

Good. I got his attention.

We had a great team, one of the best I've ever played on. The season started against a local team of mashers who beat us by a couple runs. It was the last time we lost all season. And I settled into a deliberate rhythm that carried me through the next months.

On game days they'd call us out early for dinner. After the game I'd ice my knee and slowly walk the compound, smoking a cigar. After ten o'clock count I watched late night Star Trek and ironed my khakis for the next morning, enjoying having the TV room all to myself.

I began to take pleasure in small tasks. It occurred to me that one might formulate a life along those lines. Contrary to my former, grandiose ideas, I began to understand that when one is grounded in steady habits, one is inured against troubles.

Every morning I walked the long path with Bill Spat, a guy who it turns out I'd worked in a Punk club with on Lansdowne Street in Boston right out of college. This was a different kind of walk than the evening walk. This was the when-I-get-back-in-the-world-what-I'm-gonna-do kind of walk, attempted in pairs, which gets faster each lap, gathering all the momentum of a runaway train.

After breakfast I went to work in Education. Then in the afternoon they called us out for the 500 hour Residential Drug and Alcohol Program.

(The RDAP was the Holy Grail. You started angling to get in early on, making sure to cite substance abuse problems during the court's pre-sentencing investigation.)

They posted a list on a bulletin board several months in advance of the start of your class, and a lot of fellows milled around looking for their name. It signaled the end. After completing the class you were sent to a halfway house for six months. Maybe a month into halfway house you were eligible for transfer to home confinement. In all it knocked about six months off your sentence, and you did your last six in the world.

On the first day of class I looked around the room. An assortment of foolish characters I'd seen around camp were sitting in a circle on folding metal chairs.

Willy, part Indian, was a jovial little person with coke-bottle glasses and a temper that came out of nowhere. He had been addicted to oxycontin on the street.

Miami was a short little shit who was incapable of using his native intelligence for anything besides his own survival, which probably cost a good deal of ingenuity, indeed.

Jay's personality had been beaten into shape by an alcoholic father. Of a naturally sweet disposition, he was incapable of any kind of sustained intimacy, like routine conversation, without resorting to some kind of foolery.

Vladdy had an ironic smirk set in his perpetually unshaven face. Once or twice he referred privately to the Albanian mafia. I couldn't tell if this guy was connected or entirely delusional. Despite his sense of humor, he seemed devoid of empathy; one wondered what was really going on behind that mask.

The rest I really don't remember. Most were adept at lying low. I understand their reticence. Prison does not encourage self-disclosure, making any kind of drug rehab problematic. Though we were all sentenced (and advised of a confidentiality policy which did not in fact protect us from admissions of new crimes), there was still the sensitive matter of how we might or might not have cooperated with the government. And though everybody had surely cooperated on some level—this being a camp in which the judge had ordered the coveted RDAP—no one of course admitted it; in fact, they pronounced the word *snitch* the more venomously.

Still, you could tell each man had had his reckoning, been forced to renounce his ways and nursed that raw spot like an amputee cradling the stub of an arm.

Ms. Wait, a patient, bemused woman, sat in the circle with us and introduced herself.

Jay immediately chimed in: "Wait," he said, "Wait," with Tourette's-like repetition.

Miami and Vlad sniggered.

Willy looked off somewhere.

"Yes, my name is Lori Wait. I'm a counselor and I can write you up the same as any other Corrections Officer." She stopped and let that sink in. In fact, all B.O.P. personnel had that authority. Some relished it; other's seemed abashed. She was just a teacher trying to maintain order; trying to earn a living. I saw her once in a Correction Officer's uniform, pressed into duty. A group of them were standing in a hallway preparing to toss a dormitory. As I passed by I thought she rolled her eyes.

"Cognitive Behavioral Therapy is meant to identify thinking errors." Ms. Wait continued, patiently. "Let's look at the list of *cognitive distortions.*"

"Awfulizing. All-or-nothing-thinking." I read down the list. Each seemed to hit home. I not only committed a lot of thinking errors, I embraced them, endeavored to make a virtue of them. Hadn't my "decision" to get involved in a criminal enterprise been a kind of all or nothing thinking?

"I'd like each of you to think of a personal example. Write it down in your notebook," Ms. Wait said.

Emotional reasoning: Because I feel bad, everything is bad. "The mind is calm, the street is calm." I began writing a poem.

"Jay," Ms. Wait spoke up. "What've you got?"

"Not a lot," I thought to myself.

"Huh?"

"Cognitive distortions. Name one."

"Um, awfulizing?" Jay said, looking down at his book, his blond hair hanging in front of his face.

"Good. Give me an example."

"Uhm, everything is awful?" He said looking up, revealing a child's blue eyes.

"Why?"

"Well, we're in jail?"

"That's a fact. But how does your thinking about it make it awful?"

"It's awful."

Is there anything good about it?"

"No."

"Nothing?"

"Well, I've made some friends."

"Good. So it's not all awful."

"No…."

It was going to take weeks to get this thing off the ground, I thought, trying to pay attention.

A local distillery came in to play us. It was always a trip being "the prison team." Most of the guys on the opposing team were cool. Some seemed a little put off. I'm sure they had a laugh about it with the wife afterwards over dinner.

They stayed with us for an inning or two, then we pounded them pretty good. It was the top half of the last inning, the last heat of a summer evening. Castro lobbed the ball high in the air. The batter waited. He swung. And Castro dropped in a heap like he'd been shot. Everybody just stood there while Castro writhed on the ground, the batter, too, thinking it somewhat unseemly to run to first just now. Then Ransom came running out with a towel, which turned red with blood. Castro, who'd struck me as gun-shy for a softball pitcher—he flinched all the time—kicked his feet in the dust, filled with rage at the injustice, his sorry face busted open once again.

The softball season ended, I resigned from education and took a job as night orderly, too caught up with my own thoughts to make any kind of reasonable effort in education. Each night after everyone was in bed I cleaned the break room, going back and forth with that floor buffer until the floor shined. Then in the morning I'd go to class. I'd staked out my position. I was an alcoholic. No more drinking. I didn't need any AA to tell me that. I needed to get back to life, which itched like some phantom limb.

I made it through that last winter as if sleepwalking. Then spring came once again to the Alleghenies, and I began to count the days to my release.

Halfway Home

The day came with accumulating speed, and one April morning I found myself standing in front of the camp in the rain, trying to shake the feeling I was out-of-bounds. A car came into view and pulled into the parking lot. I got in and leaned over the front seat to kiss my parents.

A mile down the road was a little hotel whose main business was as a changing room for inmates coming to or leaving camp. Inside was a chintzy lobby with a pot of burnt coffee on a side table. In their room, my father handed me a paper bag with a pair of khaki pants, a polo shirt, a belt, shoes and a light raincoat. I stripped out of my grey sweats and stuck them in the bag.

As we drove out of site I threw the bag out the car window—looked back at it lying there in the rain, depressed by the meagerness of the gesture. On the highway I glared at the unfamiliar, gray

Pennsylvania landscape, prison country, then fell into a deep sleep I can only compare to that first sleep after they arrest you.

An hour or so later I woke up and uttered a string of profanities. "What the fuck, where the hell are we?"

My dad was getting gas. I got out of the car and went into the station to buy some junk food, feeling like a lunatic escaped from the asylum.

The rest of the ride was pretty quiet, my parents mostly anxious for their son's future, no doubt; a grown man sleeping like a kid in the back seat.

Finally I began to recognize familiar landmarks of New York and Connecticut, scenes from another life, and had my parents stop at a Wild Oats (against the conditions of self-surrender). I wanted to get some stuff to bring into the halfway house, but more than that, I wanted to check back in on life. The last six years had been so squalid; I wanted to look at something nice.

At the grocery store the aisles were awhirl with shoppers. Women shot aggressively past with their carts. Everyone seemed to have something on his mind, somewhere to go. I stumbled around, lost. Then I found some toiletries and some protein bars and headed for the exit, unwittingly maneuvering into the self-checkout lane. I stood there for a moment in wonder, feeling a rush of fear, then anger, then despair at the pointless, incessant vicissitudes of life.

It was just a short drive to the halfway house now. Whatever pitched emotions I'd ridden out of Allenwood plunged me now into a trough of despond. I said goodbye to my parents and walked up a sidewalk and rang a doorbell. The halfway house was a much-abused Asylum Hill Victorian; sunlight smeared on Plexiglas windows, scuffed linoleum floors, battered moldings caked with dirt, it was an apt symbol of my life.

*

The first few days were torture. Before they let you look for a job you had to go through orientation and put in a good number of hours washing dishes and other menial tasks. The rest of the time you spent with your nose against the window like a dog waiting to be let out.

—And like a dog I went sniffing around every guy that came back, trying to figure where jobs were. Generally people were pretty unhelpful, content to keep to themselves. In spite of all the petty antipathy in jail, there's a kind of *esprit de corps* that shared suffering inspires. In a halfway house, however, everything and everyone is an obstacle, an ugly reminder and counterpoint to one's real, long-lost life beckoning one back from afar.

Finally my turn came and I filled out a card accounting for my movements that day. You had two weeks to find a job; if you didn't secure employment, it was grounds for being sent back to jail, losing good time and generally having all your dreams dashed in your face.

My first day out the door was a hot April morning. Forsythia blossoms fairly burst out of branches. I'd arranged to check out some restaurants downtown; it seemed the likeliest gig to land. As I walked up the sidewalk behind Harford Accident and Indemnity Company, down Asylum St. and under the train trestle into town, I thought of Stevens' "light masculine, / working with big hands, on the town, / arranging its heroic attitudes."

First thing I bought a cigar and hied into Bushnell Park and slinked around awhile before wandering up to the Auditorium to see a sculpture that my mother had sent me pictures of in jail— looking for some kind of affirmation, I suppose, that I was actually "out."

Cutting across the Park I avoided the businessmen on lunch break, the joggers, the young mothers with strollers and ended up at Pulaski Circle where there used to be a street where my

grandfather and his brother ran the Altone Press in the forties—
my yearning for suits and crossword puzzles and cigarette cases in-
herited from him, a typesetter and amateur boxer—and drinker,
who fetched up high and dry at last at his in-laws' house, the old
Heidelberg platen press retired to a corner of a tobacco shed where
it turned out the occasional invitation to my mom's ballet recitals.
(Our first edition of *Squid* had been printed on such a machine.)

I ate at a lunch truck, walked past a few restaurants, making
mental notes. A thunderstorm moved in later that afternoon. I had
19 minutes to get back to the halfway house.

Work

I got a job as a waiter at a French Restaurant downtown. The bar manager knew me from a long time before, so he hired me with a minimum of explanation.

Walking to work in the morning I seemed to recognize in myself ex-cons from television: *The Rockford Files*: sad and middle-aged and unfashionable in a windbreaker; on guard against vindictive parole officers, vengeful colleagues, a society with no inclination or reason to give you a second chance.

The fact is, I was nervous as hell, and I interacted with everyone in the same wooden manner I waited on tables with. One brassy redheaded waitress even walked up to me and did a karate kick in my face, saying in her way, Lighten up, dude. I appreciated the gesture, feeling the stirrings of my first crush in years.

The depressing thing about getting out of jail after all that time dreaming of getting back on the street is recognizing in oneself all the gestures of a nature essentially unchanged by experience. The discipline one learns in a jailhouse does not translate to the real world. One learns a kind of patience because there's no choice. One may even attain a kind of civic-mindedness in jail because the social and economic forces that warp one's relation to the body politic do not exist there; true, there are rigid and often violent divisions between men, but incarceration tends to have a democratizing effect. And the simple, common goal of survival renders the actions of men almost intelligible.

Things went along ok. I made pretty decent money. (You were supposed to give up a quarter of your pay, so I kept a wad of money in my locker at work.) I don't mean to give the impression that I was falling back into criminal habits; I recognized the halfway house (and the restaurant tip system) for what it was and determined to use it to get on as square a footing as possible.

One day my father drove me to get my driver's license. (At Allenwood, upon entry into the RDAP, they had you fill out paperwork for a new Social Security Card so you could get on with the business of putting your life back in order.) Since my license had expired, I had to take the driving test as well as the written test, surrounded by nervous sixteen year olds, that *Rockford Files* feeling upon me again. We got about half way up the road and the driving instructor, realizing the absurdity of our situation, told me to turn around. "You passed," he said.

Afterwards, my father said he had a stop to make before we went back to the halfway house. Then he stopped off at home, just like that: the home I'd dreamed of for half a dozen years: Lying in a jail cell on Christmas Eve, late at night, and closing my eyes and trying to conjure the deep quiet of the house. The place that sheltered me from the world. The place I always returned one last time.

As my father disappeared into the basement I walked through the kitchen, down the hallway, turned the corner to the dining room and broke into a run, sliding on the wood floor as if on hockey skates and grabbed the ball atop the newel post, launching myself onto the stairway, laughing aloud at the familiarity, seven years old now, on all fours bounding to the top step and turning the corner to my room—the room in which I'd become conscious of the world.

My father had turned it into a study of sorts—though other than an adding machine and box of invoices there was little to recommend it as a work space. Mostly it was lots of stuff from storage: mementos: high-school letters, his honorable discharge from the Marines, a wedding photo, pictures of him and my mother on bike trips, the baseball I hit for the high school record with a little homemade plaque, shelves of thrillers. He seemed to be laying his life out for review.

Above a desk pushed against the eve was a world map. I looked at the little colored pins indicating places my parents had visited, mentally overlaying my own travels, tracing with a finger that obscure, graded highway that headed north through the bush, between Benin and Nigeria, to a mystery I had once known.

I felt a need to explain how I had taken this turn; to lay some portion of my own life out for review. Though my life had diverged distinctly from my parents' lives, there was still the deep bond of father and son who had striven together out on frigid hockey rinks, or down in the dirt behind home plate in chest protector and shin guards, eleven-years old and skinny as hell, in triumph and defeat, never for a second doubting that the thing we strove for was each other's affection.

If it was justified at first, one eventually came to realize that the feelings of pitch and moment were a kind of self-flattery. The visit home was a little prelude. In a matter of weeks they released me to home confinement. This meant going to work as scheduled, returning home after a reasonable commute and making yourself available in case they wanted to call, which they did, to make sure you were home. You got about an hour a day of scheduled "recreation," which I spent walking the neighborhood at night listening to the ghosts of childhood. The rest of the time I fiddled with a new laptop.

I had a few reunions. A couple of pals drove up from New York for a cookout and some whiffle ball. A shot of bourbon.

Then L came back from the West Coast and drove down from Boston.

So this was the moment I'd been waiting for. The last time I'd seen her was at the 14th Street subway stop before my arrest as she was headed off to Hawaii. She'd cried, and I'd allowed myself to believe she was going to miss me, when the real reason she was crying was that she was thinking about leaving me for good. It's true: we'd gone off in such different directions: she tramping through wet hapu'u ferns on the summit of Kilauea in search of *Oma'o* while I wandered the lower east side of New York, poking my head into bar after bar in search of an image equal to the desolation I felt.

She never visited me in jail all those years, which suited us both because it allowed us each our privacy. Seeing me like that would have deprived us both of a certain opinion of me. Despite everything I still believed, for good or ill, that I had my reasons and despite whatever Faustian bargain I'd made for experience, those reasons were valid.

So here she was, in front of my parents' house, in a rush, looking lovely and breathless in a green sarong.

We ran into each other's arms, and then we went inside. And the little flame of industry smoldering down in my heart leapt up as a door was thrown open and a shovelful of coal thrown in.

Fired

A month or so into home confinement I managed to miss one of my N.A. meetings; the thing completely slipped my mind. I'd finished my shift at the restaurant and was stopping by the halfway house to pay a bill when they informed me I was more or less under arrest.

Unbelievable. Not to mention L was around the corner, having driven down from Boston. I was trying to explain this to the front door guard, to no avail. One of the other Community Corrections personnel seemed to get my predicament.

"So you have to go back to the restaurant *to punch out*, right?"

"Right," I stammered.

After sending L home I turned myself back in to the halfway house and went to bed around seven o'clock, curling under a thin blanket as I tried to blink it all out: the first day of jail all over again, a nightmare. The following Monday the administrative staff brought me up on charges. I had to return to the halfway house for two weeks—not the worst result considering all the horror stories I'd heard guys in camp tell about being violated for trivial infractions and sent back to prison for real, (and why some guys expressed a preference for "going to the door," rather than walk the probationary tightrope).

After getting fired from the restaurant for general ineptitude, I went to work for my brother-in-law, Larry, building houses. For the next two weeks he came by the halfway house and we'd head off in his pick-up truck, all tools, pencil stubs and dirt.

The house he was building was his personal trial. It was also *his* second act, Larry having reinvented himself as a contractor after the housing bust of the 90s destroyed first his business, then his marriage. He'd married my sister and they were expecting a baby; I'd met Larry for the first time when they came out to visit me in jail in Chicago.

My first day on the job site I climbed a staircase to the second floor. That was as far as they'd gotten: a sort of platform looking out through the trees. Larry's son was fiddling with a gas-powered nail gun; his son's pal was puking into a tree. Larry was reading a blueprint. Some contractor drove by in a truck and yelled, "Hey, finish that house!"

"Fuck you…." Larry trailed off, realizing the guy was already out of earshot.

In a couple weeks we had all the walls up, had propped up a roof beam and started running roof joists.

By the time the structure was finished it was mid-summer and time to shingle the roof. Of course the kids balked, were too hung over or scared or both. So the forty and fifty-year-old went up on the roof in a hundred degree weather to finish the job. It was brutal work, hauling fifty-pound packages of shingles over the ridgeline, the July sun beating down. As fast as Larry could shoot a shingle into the roof I had another one in his hands. I wanted to finish the job because L was coming down to visit.

Over the next months we managed to stay busy with a lot of pick-up jobs, and I went through the motions, one foot in the real world, one foot still in jail. In the process the strangest thing, the certainty that I'd somehow lost track of about a half a dozen years began to preoccupy me. It was as if those years lived in jail didn't count somehow. I kept wanting to slip back into a biological moment that had passed long ago, felt in some cellular way thirty-three years old to the day, the minute, the second they took me away.

Opening boxes of stuff salvaged from my apartment in New York was like opening little time capsules, snapshots: In the pocket of a leather coat a pair of gloves carefully folded. A bookmark in a book: Babel's *Red Cavalry*.

I went through boxes of papers, *Squid* mock-ups, photo-negatives, kitchen appliances, ruined clothes.

There was a big antique reproduction filing cabinet made of solid oak with brass fittings. I pulled at the bottom drawer, then the top; the cabinet rocked back and forth, locked tight. The keys were nowhere to be found

What the hell was in there? No money, certainly; I'd been fairly impecunious for some time, though one still dreamed of finding a stack of bills hidden away. What was so important I'd filed it away and locked it? The thing must have weighed a hundred pounds or more.

"Where's the keys for this thing, Dad?"

"I don't know," he said.

"Fuck!"

I grabbed a hammer lying on the floor and walked across the garage and swung it down onto the top of the cabinet with all my might. The wood absorbed the blow, and the hammer vibrated like a fastball on the hands. I stepped in again, intending damage. The wood split along the grain. Swung again, a glancing blow that had me off balance, staggering drunkenly.

I battered my knuckles on the edge of a molding, the torn skin pale white before the blood came rushing in. My father looked on, merely curious, approving.— Swung again, smashing a piece of molding loose. Went down on a knee now, swinging at the upright, grunting as I brought my arm back and swung, back and swung, and back and swung.

What should have been a decisive gesture dragged on for minutes, became ugly.

I tipped the cabinet over and hacked at it, knocking, at last, a hollow sound out of the thing and went at the remaining frame like a man kicking apart a paper model; finally knocked the last side over in a heap and staggered to my feet, slipping on a pile of obsolete papers, gasping for breath … and looked up at my father, eyes stinging with sweat, as if to say, *This is how it feels.*

Before long my six months was up. I'd completed home confinement and thus my term of incarceration and was transferred to probation with little fanfare.

The P.O. was a good guy. Almost immediately we established that his son played prep school ball against my *alma mater.* This guy clearly had more likely recidivists than me to deal with. If I stayed out of trouble (his words), he'd reduce my probation level over the next few weeks. In the mean time I needed to check in Monday afternoons with my pay stub from the previous week and a written request to travel outside the Connecticut district if I needed.

After I requested to go to Boston to see L four weekends in a row, he waved the restriction. (You learned early on in prison to guide your jailers onto the path of least resistance.)

It was winter now. I drove up to Cambridge and met L at a Middle Eastern Restaurant in Inman Square. We sat in a little window seat by ourselves drinking Moroccan tea. After dinner she produced a cake decorated with fondant handcuffs to celebrate my release from jail. Over the next months I'd race up after work on Friday nights and we'd go out on the town to the poshest places we could find: hotel bars and cigar lounges, chocolate buffet at the Ritz. We'd stay the weekend at her parents' place, and on Sunday night I'd drive home.

Back in Connecticut we were working on an addition overlooking the Farmington River, which had frozen solid. Shortly before Christmas a gaggle of wild turkeys flew low across the River, making a racket. I bounced a rock over the frozen surface; a series of loud pings echoed weirdly the length of the river. I sat in a snow bank drinking steaming hot tea from a thermos. I was so happy I didn't even know it.

Witness

When they called me back to Chicago to testify against Piss-Paul, I went looking for the Chicago Metropolitan Correction Center as one goes looking for the footpaths of his youth. Walking from my hotel on State Street toward Van Buren, I felt a chill go through me. Then, suddenly smaller than I expected, like a classmate once regarded with awe worn down by the years, it appeared in all its terror and foolishness.

I walked down Van Buren avoiding eye contact with the perimeter guard and slinked into the garage across the street, took the elevator to the top floor and peered out from the behind a pillar.

I counted twelve floors up and lit a cigar. Claire and Hester were in there, transferred from their cushy camps to testify, getting a real taste of jail now, and another little drama was about to be played out.— I imagined it, a voyeur once again:

When the front door buzzed, Claire walked out of her cell to see what was going on. A couple new inmates were standing at the C.O.'s desk clutching blankets and towels. In an instant she recognized Temper, who slowly turned, eyes locking on Cleary for a moment before recognizing her. An initial catch in her breath. Then a feeling of acid settling on her heart.... I would elaborate on that moment … but I was just too far to distinguish anyone; happily for inmates the life of a prison goes on in private, modestly.

I counted three floors to fifteen, my floor, and found the lit window of my old cell, and a strange thing happened: I kept imagining how I must look standing there, a grainy figure on the bare, brutalist-style garage, as if I actually *were* inside the jail, propped on an elbow, looking out. As if that view were burned onto my retina. I can still see it.

On the third day of Paul's trial I entered the courtroom through a door near the prosecutors. Paul sat hunched over in a light suit across the room with his attorneys, scowling. The last time I'd seen him was in the hotel in Jakarta. He'd come into the room with Barry, studiously avoiding eye contact. "Where's the bag?" he'd said, struggling to control his voice.

A Clerk swore me in in front of Judge Norgle. On direct examination, AUSA MacBride led me through a chronology of Paul's involvement in the conspiracy: *Yes, in fact I handed a bag of heroin to Paul in Jakarta.*

On cross, Paul's attorney undertook to fast-talk me, and I deliberately broke his rhythm by drawling my answers out: *No, I didn't actually* see *any heroin, but we did get paid $65,000 for whatever* was *inside the bag.* Afterwards, I walked down to the street, climbed the stairs to the el, got on a train for O'Hare and flew back home.

*

Alhaji eluded extradition from England to the U.S. on heroin conspiracy charges, using all his guile and money to go free. He was playing a deeper game, preparing to burn Banque International du Benin on a huge loan, abscond to Nigeria and buy his way into party politics, a would-be king-maker.

These were high times on the Lagos social scene. You wanted to be there with Alhaji dancing at the Victoria Island Hotel where Fuji singers sang his praises and where there were those who knew him as a hustler and those who know him as a pol., and those who didn't know the difference.

He'd returned to Nigeria in triumph. He'd done time and prevailed against U.S. extradition efforts; had made millions over the years, and now he was on the streets giving it away.

Dispensing autos, bags of rice, cash and kerosene to voters in the southwest of the country and submitting political rivals and allies alike to certain "fetish oaths," Alhaji and his *Omo Ilu* foundation bullied its way into the People's Democratic Party, catching first the attention of Ogun State Governor Gbenga Daniel, and then former President Olusegun Obasanjo, who urged Alhaji to run for Daniel's seat.

Alhaji instead backed Obasanjo's man Goodluck Jonathan for President. In return Jonathan made Alhaji PDP party boss of Ogun State, opening a public rift between Alhaji and Obasanjo … a dangerous man to have as an enemy, a veteran of military coups, assassination attempts and prison, who refers to his lingering moment in Nigerian history as "my watch."

When Jonathan's popularity ultimately dimmed in 2015, Alhaji promptly stepped from behind the curtain fully transformed into the Senator-elect from Ogun State East.

Before the first blush of success wore off, he seemed to sense his adversaries crowding around (as he always did—repelling rival gangs armed with rebars and small arms with the same dispatch that he thwarted political rivals) and he sued Obasanjo, the Minister of Justice, The Attorney General and National Drug Law Enforcement Agency in Federal Court for plotting with American DEA to deprive him of his freedom.

That was indeed the case when masked NDLEA agents surrounded Alhaji's house and stormed the upstairs bedroom a short time later in May 2015.

Contemporary accounts have Alhaji barricaded in his bathroom making frantic calls to lawyers. Newspaper photographs show soldiers milling about in the street behind a cordon.

A formal request for extradition had been made by the U.S. Embassy following a Seventh Circuit rejection of Alhaji's motion to dismiss charges, and the NDLEA placed Alhaji under house arrest.

The drama lasted several days. Lawyers came and went, wives brought food and medicine.

Alhaji yelled through the door that he would never let them take him….

A court finally ordered the NDLEA away, ruling that they had entered Alhaji's home illegally—allowing Alhaji to attend his political coronation two weeks later, with trepidation.

He has since taken his place in the Nigerian Senate. I imagine him in the legislative chamber throwing the sleeve of an *agbada* over his shoulders with a Roman gravitas. To date there have been no legislative achievements; mostly PDP in-fighting and numerous intrigues reported in the local tabloids.

In the wake of an appeals court decision clearing the way for Alhaji's extradition, the Ministry of Justice has asked the U.S. to submit a fresh request in order to begin proceedings.

The Supreme Court has since heard the case and somewhat mysteriously reserved judgement. And a proposed amendment to the country's extradition law has been put before the National Assembly, seemingly tailored to Alhaji's situation precisely. The law would prevent extradition "where a claim of mistaken identity is raised by a Nigerian citizen who is the defendant in an extradition case that has been concluded by any country...."

One might sense an endgame being played if one hadn't already seen it played a half-dozen times before.

It's almost strange to think of him this way, like a leopard driven out of hiding and routed through the streets; a man who moved behind a screen now waging a public relations campaign on Facebook and Wikipedia. And of course the courts. Perhaps that is exactly who he was meant to be. Perhaps king.

When the courts are all exhausted, and the prayers to Allah and the ministrations of the voodoo priests are all exhausted, and the "twenty men or more" and the crooked cops and all the borders across which one flees have been exhausted ... will one still have one last move to play?

The World

As for everyone else, each person returned to some unfinished version of himself. Claire went back to Cincinnati. One night sitting on the couch in PJs with her momma she found herself watching a likeness of herself on a TV prison drama. Temper was a celebrity now, attending galas and advising Senate sub-committees about prison reform after writing a book-turned-TV-show about her skid-bid in Danbury—in which her former lover, Claire, was portrayed. And the tabloids got interested for a couple months in ironing out the pillow talk. Who said what and made love to whom.

Hester found Jesus.

Brad died. I had no contact with him after we got arrested or after I got out and we were both living our lives again. His obituary says he'd been living in Western Pennsylvania (near where he was from on the Ohio-West Virginia border), and working as a chef.

Condolences by former classmates, cousins and recent colleagues evoke the same joyful person everyone knew.

If I may be permitted to compose a last image of Brad—with veiled black pillbox and lipstick, skipping around the room in high heels and a bottle of Heineken because as always it was going to be the greatest night of our lives—I do so with utter trepidation. I brought a misery into his life.

I continued to have dreams about smuggling, blazing routes across an impossibility of time zones and geographies.... The dreams came and went, sometimes staying for a week at a time like bad weather, tokening nothing in themselves except moods.

I finished with the construction job and moved up to Cambridge. I'd gotten a job at a small private college as an adjunct professor, and L and I moved into an apartment in Porter Square, a little aerie on the third floor of a pre-Civil War building on Linnaean Street overlooking great cake-like clapboard mansions. Each morning I'd walk down Mass. Avenue to the edge of Harvard Square in autumnal sunshine and frost, take a bus to Cleveland Circle and walk the tree-lined streets up to the college in a reverie of disbelief—the sounds and accents of prison still reverberating in my ears as I stood before class, straining slightly at an academic register.

I found myself a local coffee shop, bookstore, barber shop, tobacconist, park bench and bar where I drank cokes and listened to the locals quip about the old towne team on sultry, slow evenings all through the summer, enjoying semi-anonymity as long as it would last—for eventually they recognize you've been sitting there and demand you make an accounting of yourself.

Eventually, I became one of the crowd. Spread out into the state college system, commuting to Framingham, Salem and Quincy; and L and I got married on a lovely May day in New England and honeymooned in Costa Rica, my first time abroad in years;

and finally mastering my life again, we up and moved to Volcano, Hawaii, a Federal Judge in Massachusetts granting early termination, and retired for a time 4000 feet atop Kilauea in towering hapu'u ferns and ohia, raising chickens and splitting wood and writing some tentative things, and letting everything settle, settle, settle as I sat in the late, deep afternoons, rude, eager, rasped sounds of life rising along the long flank of the volcano like smoke in the fading February light, which shone sulfurous from behind the massive structure of Mauna Loa, then green, then puce for an aching instant, like the edges of a bruise on the third day when everything looks a lot worse than it really is.

CPSIA information can be obtained
at www.ICGtesting.com
Printed in the USA
FSHW012057290119
55357FS